Small Firms in Global Competition

International Business Education
and Research Program

Small Firms in Global Competition

Edited by
TAMIR AGMON
RICHARD DROBNICK

A Research Book from
the International Business Education
and Research Program
University of Southern California

BIP 00

New York   Oxford
OXFORD UNIVERSITY PRESS
1994

Oxford University Press

Oxford   New York   Toronto
Delhi   Bombay   Calcutta   Madras   Karachi
Kuala Lumpur   Singapore   Hong Kong   Tokyo
Nairobi   Dar es Salaam   Cape Town
Melbourne   Auckland   Madrid

and associated companies in
Berlin   Ibadan

Published by Oxford University Press, Inc.,
200 Madison Avenue, New York, New York 10016

Oxford is a registered trademark of Oxford University Press

Library of Congress Cataloging-in-Publication Data
Small firms in global competition /
edited by Tamir Agmon, Richard Drobnick.
p.   cm.
"A research book from the International Business Education and
Research Program, University of Southern California."
Includes bibliographical references and index.
ISBN 0-19-507825-X
1. Small business—Management.   2. Small business—Finance.
3. Competition, International.   I. Agmon, Tamir.   II. Drobnick, Richard.
III. University of Southern California.
International Business Education and Research Program.
HD62.7.S613   1994   658.02'2—dc20   92-40074

2 4 6 8 9 7 5 3 1

Printed in the United States of America
on acid-free paper

To Dana, Tali, and Gregory
—tomorrow's global competitors

Preface

As trade barriers fall and mergers and alliances proliferate, the line between domestic and foreign firms becomes increasingly blurry. Ford owns Jaguar, Chrysler owns Lamborghini, while Honda is made in America. As Professor Mark Weinstein put it, "Globalization is like Muhammad Ali's right fist: You can run, but you can't hide." Until quite recently, however, studies of globalization have tended to focus on industrial giants—the Exxons, the AT&Ts, the Sonys, and the Mitsubishis. The message has been that "global" is synonymous with "giant," and that globalization requires size, to achieve economies of scale, and therefore also requires a product that will be all things to all people.

Little has been done to help CEOs of small to midsize firms think about what is necessary to change their corporate strategies from local to global, despite the fact that examples of successful international businesses operating on a more modest scale are common: Christian Dior fashions, Movado watches, Nike shoes. Paradoxically, with the right product in the right niche, smallness may be not a liability, but an asset. And since small to midsize companies have historically been the engines of innovation and growth in local economies, there is reason to believe that they can provide the same function internationally.

This book, covering both theory and practice, and representing the work of several of the most respected voices in the field of international business, is aimed at those executives of small to midsize companies who have been ignored in most discussions of globalization. Its purpose is to provide a useful starting place for American managers of less-than-huge corporations who know that change is necessary, but are not sure where to start.

Each author speaks from his or her own expertise, and taken together they reflect the two opposing forces seen in today's headlines. Some think that the world is moving toward a single global market. Others think it is moving toward three markets—the American (dominated by the United States), the European Community (dominated by

Germany), and the Asian (dominated by Japan). In truth, the tug-of-war between the world views of homogeneity and heterogeneity is likely to continue into the next century, until it becomes clear that both trends will coexist.

The book is also a potent argument against current sentiments that suggest the United States is no longer a world-shaping economic force. It is true that the U.S. demand for imports and the stagnation of American exports between 1981 and 1985 created huge trade deficits. As Americans increased personal consumption and reduced personal savings (without any substantial change in business savings and investment rates), the financing needs of a deficit-ridden American government had to be met by foreign creditors. This produced the anomalous situation of the world's richest nation borrowing and attracting investment capital from poorer nations to such an extent that from 1984 to 1992 the United States transformed itself from a net $164 billion capital export position to a net $462 billion capital import position. Unfortunately, this inflow of foreign capital did not increase America's investment rate as a share of GNP.

Nevertheless, by 1986, the competitive effects of the dollar depreciation had started to work, and merchandise exports from the United States began a phenomenal expansion. In part this was due to the steadily improving competitiveness of the U.S. manufacturing sector, where unit labor costs declined from 1982 to 1990 by 3.5 percent, as compared to a 2.5 percent decline for Japan, a 17 percent increase for Germany, and a 22 percent increase for France. In inflation-adjusted terms, between 1987 and 1991, exports of U.S. goods and services grew at an annual average rate of about 10 percent, while imports only rose half as fast.

The trade improvement of the past five years is likely to continue for the following reasons:

- The October 1990 budget agreement and the peace dividend will reduce America's savings-investment imbalance.
- The current and expected dollar exchange rate will cause goods made in America to continue to be price competitive.
- Manufacturing productivity growth is likely to continue to match or exceed wage growth.
- Income growth in America's trading partners is likely to exceed U.S. income growth.
- American firms will continue to become motivated to export, given slow growth in the U.S. market and the international price competitiveness of their products.
- America's trading partners will be under continuous pressure to open their markets as negotiators in the Commerce Department and the U.S. Trade Representative's office continue to acquire

more influence in U.S. government interagency debates in the aftermath of the collapse of the Soviet Union.

Stabilization of the international economic system requires an expansion of exports from America and a slowing—if not an actual reduction—of imports into America. This change will shape the business environment and will cause more American firms, large and small, to look overseas for growing markets.

American leaders must rid themselves of the self-crippling mind-set that says America does not have enough resources to influence and shape international events. America is a rich, productive nation that can make a number of choices to release resources in order to shape the international economic environment.

Without waiting for government action, American business leaders should begin now to invest in their current and future employees to make them smarter about international economics, politics, and culture. Relative to their foreign competitors, American managers are substantially less competent to think in terms of numerous currencies, numerous legal systems, and numerous political and cultural barriers to the flow of ideas, raw materials, and products. That must change.

This book is intended as one step in that direction.

Acknowledgment

This work was funded in part by the U.S. Department of Education under a Title VI-B grant.

Los Angeles   Richard Drobnick
December 1992   Judith Garwood

Contents

Part I Globalization: Should You Do It?

What are the principal conditions necessary for successful global operations of small firms? First, identify a product and a market in a non-global industry, one in which more than a small number of giant firms can operate, and one that does not require economies of scale. Then, dominate a niche. This chapter includes several examples of successful global strategies of small and medium-sized firms in different industries and analyzes the necessary entry strategies.

Part II Changing Your Mind-Set, Changing Your Strategy

A useful way to start thinking of strategic change is to divide the business environment into local markets and global markets and to analyze the differences between the two. For example, in global markets, the importance of customer relationships may be weaker, the production process may be simpler, and the competition more intense. This analysis forms a base for rethinking and restructuring the relationship between the corporate strategy and the environment.

verting funds that could be used more productively in research and development, and second, by artificially sheltering the firms from their very real international competition.

Kathleen K. Reardon and Robert Spekman

An alliance with another company eases somewhat the need for a firm to do all things well in two different cultures, particularly if the new relationship is skillfully managed from the initial handshake onward. This chapter discusses, with specific case examples, the problems of establishing trust, rapport, and mutually agreed-upon expectations across cultural barriers, ending with guidelines for developing a negotiation strategy.

Part IV Practical Applications

Gerhard Plenert

The choice of a planning and control system for a factory depends on what resource you want to use most efficiently (in the United States it is usually labor, in Japan it is usually materials) and what the primary corporate goals are (only in the United States, Canada, and Europe are they likely to be financial). So the "world model" for manufacturing is not a model with a single perfect answer, but one that looks specifically at a particular factory in terms of its resource focus and its goals, which must be harmonious with those of the employees, the government, and the culture.

Ben M. Bensaou

If communicating between companies within one culture can sometimes be difficult, managing new relationships across national boundaries requires a quantum leap. The author suggests that the coordination problems are reduced as the conditions that produce uncertainty (the conditions of partnership, task, and environment) are eased. He illustrates his point with a study of the changing buyer-supplier relationships in the U.S. and Japanese automotive industries.

Mary B. Teagarden, Mark C. Butler, and Mary Ann Von Glinow

To seek a competitive edge, firms in industrialized countries frequently look off shore for a way to reduce labor and other factor costs.

Many American firms have been looking to Mexico, an alternative that the authors clearly see as a good bargain. They examine the pluses and minuses of a *maquiladora* plant, and then offer some thoughtful management advice for the corporate executives who find themselves bridging cultures.

Privatization of industry in Eastern Europe has created an overwhelming need for capital to support new small and midsize firms. These are the businesses that lead innovation and productivity in any type of economy, and countries such as Hungary are offering liberal policies and attractive tax holidays to encourage foreign direct investment and joint ventures.

Contributors

TAMIR AGMON
University of Southern California
Tel Aviv University

YAIR AHARONI
Tel Aviv University

JERRY L. ARNOLD
University of Southern California

BEN M. BENSAOU
INSEAD

MARK C. BUTLER
San Diego State University

PAULA J. CAPRONI
University of Michigan

RICHARD DROBNICK
University of Southern California

DAN ELNATHAN
University of Southern California

JUDITH GARWOOD
Freelance writer and editor

MICHAEL V. GESTRIN
University of Toronto

CHRISTINE R. HEKMAN
Claremont Graduate School

STEFANIE ANN LENWAY
University of Minnesota

CATHERINE L. MANN
Federal Reserve Board

THOMAS P. MURTHA
University of Michigan

GERHARD PLENERT
Brigham Young University

KATHLEEN K. REARDON
University of Southern California

ALAN M. RUGMAN
University of Toronto

ROBERT SPEKMAN
University of Virginia

MARY B. TEAGARDEN
San Diego State University

MARY ANN VON GLINOW
University of Southern California

MARK WEINSTEIN
University of Southern California

Small Firms in Global Competition

1

Comparative Advantage and Competitive Advantage: An Introduction

TAMIR AGMON
RICHARD L. DROBNICK

Two major trends have dominated the international business environment in the last twenty years. One is market integration, with global markets forming in many industries and services. The other is the emergence of large international corporations as the main actors in those markets.

Much of the research in international business has focused on these large multinational enterprises and the way they are managed, resulting in an absence of literature about the activities of the growing number of small and medium-sized firms that are active players in global markets. Some academics have even argued that in the new world of one global market (or three major regional ones), smaller firms have no role. But small and medium-sized firms account for a substantial amount of international trade, even though much of it is done through the large multinationals. In fact, there are advantages in being a relatively small firm in today's international market.

The basic concept in international trade theory is that of comparative advantage, the premises of which have remained the same since the days of Adam Smith and David Ricardo. Trade flows occur as a result of comparative advantage, and every country has comparative advantages in some economic activities. This theory has been widely discussed, and some sources for reference are listed at the end of the chapter. Within the context of neoclassical economic theory, four models of trade between countries have been developed: the Exchange Model, the Comparative Cost Model (also known as the Ricardian model), the Specific Factor Model, and the Factor Intensity Model (the Hecksher-Ohlin model). They should be viewed as developmental, in that each consecutive model includes to some extent the earlier one.

Countries do not trade, however; companies do! And just as a country has *comparative* advantages, a firm—large or small—has *competitive* advantages. The four economic models of trade that describe the sources of a nation's comparative advantage can also be used to categorize the sources of potential competitive advantage for firms.

The Four Models of International Trade Theory

In the simple Exchange Model, countries trade only their natural resources. Thus, the comparative advantage of Saudi Arabia is based on oil, while that of Chile is based on copper. While oil and copper are primary endowments, placed by nature, a nation can develop secondary endowments. Cocoa in Ghana, bananas in Nicaragua, and oil palms in Malaysia are some examples. But even in the Exchange Model, these are only potential comparative advantages. They need to be transformed or activated by people. Many large multinationals, such as oil companies and major agricultural commodities companies, base their competitive advantage on the Exchange Model.

Ricardo's Comparative Cost Model focuses on the labor unit cost of production as the key determinant for the international flow of goods. The export of labor-intensive goods like apparel from many Asian countries to the United States and the European Community is an example of this model at work. Conclusions from the Ricardian model can also be used to explain much of the export-led development plans for rebuilding the economies of Poland, Estonia, and some of the republics that once comprised the USSR. The business version of the same idea is international sourcing.

The Comparative Cost Model is based on the assumption that labor is the only factor of production. In some industries, this is a reasonable working assumption. In more complex situations, the Specific Factor Model is needed.

The Specific Factor Model assumes that firms employ two factors of production: one specific (immovable) and one freely traded. In the classical rendering, the specific factor was land, the tradable one labor. The use of Mexican labor in the development of California agriculture is a well-known example. The *maquiladora* firms discussed in Chapter 11 provide another example. In the case of these U.S.–Mexican ventures, the specific factor of production is a combination of U.S. management and access to the U.S. market, while the traded factor is again Mexican labor.

In general, it is useful to think of the specific factor as the set of unique competitive assets of the firm, with all other factors freely traded and bought in a competitive international market. Some alliances between small firms and large multinational organizations, where the former provide specific factors and the latter the international system in which they can be efficiently utilized, can be explained by the Specific Factor model. This way to facilitate the competitive advantage of small firms in a global market is discussed in Chapter 2.

The fourth model of economic trade theory is the Factor Intensity Model, developed by Heckscher and Ohlin. This model focuses on the way in which a concerted effort in research and development, marketing development, and managerial efforts in general may create a unique factor intensity that results in high wages and high return on capital. (The so-called "New Trade Theory" also uses the concept of comparative advantage as a dynamic policy variable, explaining how a country can change the nature of its factors of production by national policy choices.)

A good example of a country that has changed its comparative advantage is South Korea. In the early 1970s, South Korea's factor intensity was tilted toward low-skilled labor. The country exported apparel, simple electronic consumer goods, and basic assembly work. The corporate sector focused on labor-intensive production. But the Korean government, in cooperation with the industrial and business establishment, decided to change the structure of the economy. Thus, the focus of Korean managers had to shift from production issues to more complex ones, such as creating and developing their own research and development centers, their own brand names, and their own marketing channels. The firms made, and financed, substantial investments.

The transformation of South Korea required a tremendous effort. To be successful, the individuals guiding the change to high-skilled labor needed to create a system of shared values and shared meaning. That is, they had to change the "mind-set," or vision, of the business and political leaders. The importance of changing the corporate mind-set is discussed in Chapter 4.

The Competitive Advantage of Small and Midsize Firms

Taken together, these four models provide a way of viewing how the sources for comparative advantages of nations can be used to create competitive advantages for firms. More specifically, there are four possible sources for competitive advantage of small and midsize American firms. The two key words are identification and development: identification of a potential competitive advantage and development of the potential into a business reality.

In terms of the Exchange Model, some small companies may possess a unique endowment that gives them a monopoly position. It may be based on natural resources, specialized marketing channels, brand image, or past research and development. These cases require maintenance rather than development management, at least until new competitors threaten the status quo.

The Comparative Cost Model is the basis of international sourcing. For example, small and medium-sized U.S. firms that anticipated changes in comparative unit labor costs between the United States and Japan when the yen began to appreciate in 1985 were able to realize new business opportunities. The transfer of Japanese automobile factories to the United States opened the way for a substantial number of smaller American firms to become suppliers of various parts and services to the Japanese auto transplants.

Still, the full business potential of the changing macroeconomic circumstances is seldom captured by firms. Chapters 9 and 10 address some of the practical problems that companies have to solve.

Applying the Specific Factor Model to business requires extending the economic definition of specific factors. In the classical model, land or other physically immovable factors of production were regarded as specific to a given nation. In business practice today, management can be regarded as a specific factor for a given firm. For example, in a 1974 study, T. Horst found that the competitive edge of General Foods in the international markets could be explained only by the interface between its management and organization. This hard-to-define combination of managerial practices, accumulated experience, and organizational culture produced a unique advantage that helped General Foods to penetrate the global market successfully.

The importance of this type of specific factor is that it results from a managerial decision to succeed. It takes time to attain and needs constant maintenance in the face of competition, but it is a very real source of competitive advantage.

The Factor Intensity Model builds on the basic idea of the Specific Factor Model. What counts is the relative strength of factors or a unique combination of factors. For example, Cypress Semiconductors created a competitive edge based on a continuous research and development effort in high-performance electronic chips *combined* with an ability to identify and effectively sell in market segments (niches).

While the last two examples deal with large U.S. corporations, the approach has potential for small and midsize firms as well. In fact, it may be easier to create a cohesive and effective organizational culture in a small company. The ever-growing specialization in all industries and services opens up opportunities for small and midsize firms to find their own unique combination of product and market.

REFERENCES

Heckscher, E., "The Effect of Foreign Trade on the Distribution of Income," *Ekonomisk Tidskrift*, Vol. 21, 1919.

Horst, T., *At Home Abroad: A Study of Domestic and Foreign Operations of the American Food Processing Industry*, Bullinger, 1974.

Jones, R. W., *International Trade: Essays in Theory*, Amsterdam: North Holland, 1979.

Meade, J., *The Stationary Economy*, Allen and Unwin, 1965.

Ohlin, B., *Interregional and International Trade*, Harvard University Press, 1933.

Ricardo, D., *The Principles of Political Economy and Taxation*, Cambridge University Press, 1981.

PART I
Globalization: Should You Do It?

Small and midsize firms can develop a unique competitive advantage in the global market. As was shown in Chapter 1, a firm's specific competitive advantage can be found and developed with the help of insights about factor combinations gained from international trade theory.

In the following chapter, Yair Aharoni discusses how to create firm-specific competitive advantages by drawing on the field of corporate strategy. He maps the environment of the global market and charts alternative routes for management. The possible strategies revolve around differentiation and fit. The chosen strategy may be based on cooperation with a large multinational organization, and in some cases may even be based on an adversarial relationship, but a strategy that will create a monopolistic competitive position in some dimension is necessary. Small and midsize firms must find their own unique way and then must do a consistently superior job in realizing their choice!

2

How Small Firms Can Achieve Competitive Advantage in an Interdependent World

YAIR AHARONI

Small firms play a larger role in the economy than is often realized. Close to 90 percent of American firms employ fewer than twenty persons, and almost half the work force is employed by companies with fewer than 500 employees. In smaller countries, an even larger percentage of the work force is employed by small firms. More important, these smaller organizations are creating the new employment opportunities, not their bigger, better-known counterparts. The number of these firms that have cast their eyes beyond the domestic market may come as a surprise: A survey conducted for the Small Business Administration showed that 37 percent of the U.S. firms with fewer than 500 employees are exporting overseas, and that one quarter of all exporting companies, or more than 16,000, employ fewer than 100 people.

Since World War II, international trade has increased dramatically, and foreign direct investments (FDIs) have proliferated. Traded goods, money, information, labor, and services have all leaped over national boundaries and markets. Domestic producers who had enjoyed the luxury of a highly protected home market find themselves facing direct competition from foreign-owned, much larger, multinational enterprises (MNEs), with better reputations and lower costs, resulting from economies of scale and of scope, as well as global scanning systems for cheaper and better sources of labor, vendors, materials, parts, and sub-assemblies. Accelerated technological diffusion, integration of capital markets, reduced information and transportation costs, and liberalization of trade barriers have all combined to increase the extent and intensity of global interdependence. At the same time, in many industries power has shifted from manufacturers to giant distribution chains of mass merchandisers.

These trends are often seen as giving preference in the future global market to the giant firm, reducing the future role of small business or even questioning its ability to survive in a globally interdependent world. I propose to explore some ways in which a small business can compete effectively not only in the domestic economy, but also internationally.

Several points must be clarified. First, unfortunately, the term *firm* is ambiguous and is used in at least two meanings. One is for an autonomous, independently operated, and homogeneous business unit. Another is in the legal sense of a corporation. To avoid such an ambiguity, I shall use the term *business* or *business unit* (BU) for the first sense, and the term *company* or *corporation* for a legal, often diversified, entity.

Second, the small business units must operate in a developed environment and enjoy adequate infrastructure, such as telephones, roads, transportation, market information facilities, fax, and so on. The infrastructure is inadequate in many developing nations, and the lack of such services inhibits corporations there from competing in the world market.

Finally, the subject of analysis is the small business (and I am not offering a rigorous definition of "small") without regard to the size of the domestic market.

Background: The Globalization of Markets

The transportation revolution of the mid-19th century created the beginning of multinational competition. The communication and information revolution created the global competition we see today. Technology and information flow quickly across national boundaries. Markets for products develop almost simultaneously around the world. The need to achieve lower costs and to amortize the high fixed costs of research and development, design, production, marketing, and services is often cited as a reason to globalize. Ted Levitt argues as well that globalization is inevitable because customers' needs are becoming homogenized, and people are willing to sacrifice their first preferences in product features, design, and functions in order to pay a lower price for their second choice.

In a global industry, by definition, the relevant structure that determines behavior and competitive advantage is a worldwide one, or at least one covering the major developed markets of the world. Strategic positioning of the competitors in major national markets is fundamentally affected by their overall global positions. Therefore, firms in global industries may cross-subsidize different markets in order to achieve market share or to threaten a competitor. A major player in a global industry must build and maintain global infrastructure. This requires daunting expenditures for advertising, massive investments in sales force and distribution systems, and cost reduction by international sourcing. It also requires the ability to acquire, maintain, and deploy large-scale physical and human resources. Therefore, it is assumed, only a handful of giant corporations can compete in a global industry.

Most researchers have concentrated their attentions on the giant MNEs, neglecting the impact of global forces on small businesses. But there are small business units—not sheltered by government protection— prospering in the international marketplace and enjoying competitive advantage. Here is a look at some possible strategies.

Bases for Competitive Advantage in a World Market

There are several sources of sustainable competitive advantage. The first is the presence of a fertile climate for certain crops or the existence of certain minerals. The business unit gains a cost advantage from the accessibility of low-cost raw materials. A second is the availability of skilled workers earning low wages. For example, in low-priced denim jeans, wage labor costs are the major competitive factor, because the most labor-intensive part of the cost structure—cutting and assembly— is also the most significant. Low-cost labor suppliers from countries such as Hong Kong and South Korea have at least a 30 percent cost advantage over European producers. Large MNEs compete by sourcing from the low-cost countries.

Competitive advantage can be the result of an innovation, or of specific knowledge or skills. The invention of a safe method to ship elemental bromine in bulk gave the Israeli-based firm Dead Sea Bromine a significant technological lead over competitors who still had to ship in small containers. A very efficient process technology derived from the need to change products frequently in a small market allowed an Israeli food manufacturer to export soups in relatively small quantities, selling them as private brands to medium-sized supermarket chains.

Innovation may also allow business to realize a price premium. Price premium can also be achieved by tailoring basic equipment or software to a customer's specific needs, by offering a special product quality or unique capabilities, by supplying more convenient distribution or better service, or by creation of a brand name. More generally, a price premium may be possible because of higher quality, better design innovation, better and faster service, prompt delivery, as well as special relations with customers.

If a small BU focuses and specializes in a sophisticated product for which world demand is limited, it is able to develop firm-specific advantages and to nurture them into globally competitive advantages. Thus, if a BU focuses on the hard metals business, or on a specialized water planting device used where water is scarce and costly, it may dominate the world market—without being a giant—and be competitive.

Price premium can also be achieved by having an advantage in marketing. Hong Kong and South Korea still have a significant advantage in the labor-intensive production of high-priced denim jeans. But they face a major cost disadvantage in marketing and distribution, which account for a much more significant portion of total costs because of the larger outlay for advertising, promotion, and selling through specialized outlets (versus department stores). The clothing industry also includes businesses that specialize in design and subcontract the manufacturing, which gives corporations such as Liz Claiborne, Anne Klein, and Yves St. Laurent their advantage. Benneton has design skills and an integrative worldwide strategy. Nike offers the same in sport shoes.

Small businesses may not be able to compete when large expenditures for the establishment of a brand name are needed unless they establish strategic alliances. And they must choose carefully when looking for a base for a price premium: The cost of achieving this varies in different parts of the value chain. An advantage in design, for example, takes fewer resources than an advantage in marketing.

Firm Size, Competitive Advantage, and Industry Characteristics

It is generally assumed in economic and strategic literature that large firms enjoy a competitive advantage over small ones because they command more resources, they can control a higher market share, they can ride the experience curve faster, they enjoy strong bargaining power with suppliers and customers, and they can make more mistakes without going belly up. Indeed, several research studies have demonstrated a significant positive association between firm size and profits—from which the researchers concluded there was a causal relationship between size and profitability. A plethora of studies have also shown the importance of market share as a determinant of profitability.

Any observation of the profits of various firms in the same industry would show significant differences. Persistent high profits, unless they are explained by an accounting error, must be the result of some competitive advantage, or the consequence of a strategy. For quite a long time, industrial organization economists believed that so-called abnormal profits could be fully explained by tacit collusion or other monopoly behavior, allowing for economies of scale, brand loyalties through advertising, and barriers to entry. Most of the higher barriers to entry are associated with large corporations and are considered to be the property of a particular collection of firms called an industry. However, in several industries, such as real estate, some firms enjoy what an economist would see as persistent windfall profits that cannot be explained by predation, monopoly, collusion, or deterrence. Instead, these firms have some specific—and induplicable—assets that allow them to get high rent.

Strategy theory may be more useful in defining the basis for competitive advantage. Studies show that the key factors of success in each and every industry change as the industry evolves. At the emerging stage·of an industry, technology is a key factor of success. A small business can start with a brilliant product, develop it, and achieve rapid growth once the start-up phase has passed. Customers may doubt the ability of a tiny company to meet delivery dates and after-sale service demands, but they may be attracted by the new features. As the industry matures, cost considerations become dominant, and scale may be more important. Small BUs may not be able to compete at this stage, especially when markets are homogeneous, standardized, and large.

Industries may also be viewed according to the number of rivals. In fragmented industries, no dominant competitor exists. Since the industry is populated by a large number of small and medium-sized corporations, no business has a significant market share, and none can strongly influence the industry outcome. Entry and exit from the industry may be relatively easy, and the turnover high. These industries are characterized by absence of economies of scale, or even by diseconomies of scales, high transportation costs, and high product diversity.

In a fragmented industry, a single competitor may be able to achieve dominance if it can standardize the products or components of the products and achieve economies of scale in manufacturing, distribution, or service. Competitors may also achieve higher value-added by specialization in product type, segment, customer type, or geographic areas.

The Small Business in a Domestic Setting

A widely held view is that the right prescription for a small business in a domestic market is to avoid direct competition against the giants. This is possible in one of several ways. The first is to concentrate activities in fragmented industries.

The second is to pursue a niche strategy, concentrating in those niches that are of little or no interest to the giants—for example, by customizing to individual users who are willing and able to pay a premium rather than accept the standard version.

A third possible strategy for small BUs is to take high risks. In researching such a strategy, one has to look for special managerial characteristics, such as what David McClelland has described as the need for achievement, or other personality attributes.

Fourth, small firms also enjoy a much higher level of output flexibility than their large competitors; conversely, they are more vulnerable to changes in the environment. Large size is less of an advantage in an environment characterized by fluctuating demand than in a stable environment. Other sources of flexibility allow small BUs not only to survive but even to command abnormal profits. Short internal communication lines, for example, allow much faster response to changes in customer tastes or environmental conditions. And in a small business it is much easier to identify the person responsible for changes and build the reward system accordingly.

A fifth possibility is that the BU is a satellite unit, dependent on either a single corporation or a group of large corporations in an industry. For example, the BU may supply a large department store private brand or be a long-term supplier to a large corporation, as in the Kanban system. Toyahiro Kuno notes that a Japanese car manufacturer buys 75 percent of its parts from outside quasi-integrated suppliers. Long-term contracts shelter small BUs from risk and significantly reduce marketing costs. A variant of this strategic choice is the creation of a strategic alliance or a network of small businesses, to reduce training costs, to mitigate marketing expenditures, or to allow the scale needed to create and sustain a brand name.

Finally, a small business may be based on a major innovation and may grow to be a large business at a later stage. Sony was established by two partners in 1946 and is now a multibillion dollar diversified company. The same is true of Hewlett Packard, Apple, and a score of other firms. Of course, many more small corporations never made it or went bankrupt when the first idea was not enough to sustain a competitive advantage.

One characteristic of the 1980s, as noted, is the proliferation of global operations and global industries. This means that a small business must be able to compete in its domestic economy against giant MNEs—intruders attempting to penetrate the market. It may also choose to compete by exporting to other markets, by licensing, or through foreign direct investment.

The Small BU in a Global Market

In the world markets, as in the domestic market, competitive advantage can be gained as a result of either lower costs or a price premium. Small businesses (in world terms) can be successful when they focus on and dominate specific market niches.

There are several problems with the niche strategy, however. One is the limitation imposed on growth of the BU. If the niche does not grow, neither does the BU, unless it diversifies to other businesses, with all the coordination and control problems that entails. If the niche grows too fast, however, it will attract large competitors with massive cash outlays and extensive marketing and managerial resources. Then, too, if the technology becomes widely available, barriers to entry are reduced, and the pioneer business may find it difficult to maintain market position.

Hence, the ability to focus is a necessary but not sufficient condition for success. A small exporting BU must choose a small number of segments in which it intends to establish strength—and pursue that strength relentlessly. This specialization must not involve high research and development costs, an expensive distribution system, or the creation and maintenance of worldwide service capabilities. The giant MNEs have a clear advantage in their ability to amortize staggering R&D costs in the face of a brief product life cycle.

The core technologies used by the small business must be different enough so that they are not part of those used by giants, or the market must be small enough so that the giants will not be attracted. Since the small business cannot sustain a large sales force, the size of a typical transaction must be large, either because of a high cost per unit or because the sale is made to a large distributor on a private brand basis. Small businesses are at their best when they sell to a small number of sophisticated customers who buy quality, or to customers who need frequent changes or a specialized product and are willing to pay a price premium.

Diamonds are an example of a product with low transportation costs, little economy of scale in processing, and no need for cash outlays for R&D, for servicing, or for heavy machinery. And diamond cutting and polishing is in fact dominated by small businesses—a few small countries, notably Belgium and Israel (but also India and the USSR), have been able to maintain a significant presence in world trade through a very large number of extremely small companies. (Raw diamonds, however, are controlled by a worldwide syndicate.)

Small businesses often take too long getting a product to market, and once in the market do not grow fast enough. Even world-leading technology is not sufficient for success unless a full-scale marketing effort is launched, and this effort may be beyond the means of a small business. A small business must also develop scanning mechanisms to learn about future customers' needs. And a small business faces high risks. These problems can be solved by being part of a larger portfolio, based either on ownership or some other collaborative arrangement.

The Small BU and the Small Corporation

There is an important distinction between small BUs and small corporations. A small BU may be acquired by a large, diversified firm but still retain its character and autonomy, depending on the need for flexibility and the size of the world market. One example is Dexter Corporation. Its 1978 long-range plan states:

> Most of the products produced by Dexter are classified as specialty materials, rather than commodities, because they are formulated or designed to perform a specific, vital function in the manufacturing process of Dexter customers or in their end products. These specialty materials are not sold in the high volumes normally associated with commodity business.
> Dexter specialty materials require a high degree of technical service on an individual customer basis. The value of these specialty materials stems not just from their raw materials composition, but from the results and performance they achieve in actual use.

Dexter is divided into twenty-six strategic business segments, each one of which is quite small and very specialized. One BU produces nonwoven paper for tea bags; another, liquid epoxy coating.

Large corporations indeed have advantages that small ones do not possess. It is easier for large corporations to fund new businesses or revive faltering ones from the earnings of healthy business units. It is easier to attract skilled labor and to realize economies of scope across businesses in costs like R&D, marketing, or advertising. A major advantage is the ability to reduce risk by diversification. For small businesses, the means of spreading risks are very important. A large corporation can consist of a portfolio of small BUs, but other means of risk spreading are possible.

One possibility, therefore, is that the world is moving toward a concentration in the number of corporations, but these corporations would allow small BUs to maintain their autonomy. The large corporation may concentrate on financial decisions, provide access to markets, decide on new avenues for R&D, and maintain quality control to assure the prospective customer that certain standards of reliability are maintained.

Small corporations can of course continue to exist in fragmented industries. They can also continue to operate if the national government protects the domestic market from foreign competition. Even in these cases, successful small corporations find themselves enmeshed in competition with large MNEs. Unless they join the MNEs, they must find the means—the competitive advantage—to compete against them.

The government of a country may wish to help local firms gain access to a global giant. In return for a large government order, say engines for the air force, the MNE might agree to develop domestic vendors for its procurement requirements, promising to use its best efforts or even agreeing to commit itself for a certain amount in domestic purchases. Since business strategy is generally based on a stream of resource commitments, once the MNE familiarized itself with a certain vendor, it might continue working with that vendor (provided it received good quality products and prompt delivery) even after the offset agreement ended.

Other than becoming a part of an MNE, or an independent contractor dependent on an MNE for orders, the only alternative for the small corporation is to develop risk-sharing mechanisms on new products and markets, and to foster collaboration in R&D and marketing. A number of autonomous corporations can unite in one brand name, as is the case with regard to New Zealand kiwi growers or Danish furniture makers. Small corporations can also combine their purchasing power in procuring certain goods through a shared corporation. Pharmacies in Israel use this method.

Collaboration and Risk Sharing

If a small BU does not operate under the umbrella of a larger MNE, it must develop other means to scan the environment and be known to customers. The future means of collaboration and risk sharing are not very clear, but some speculations may be relevant.

Developments in information technologies may allow more collaboration among small BUs, obviating the need for ownership relations as part of a large corporation. For example, one advantage of an international hotel system is in reservations—customers have easy access plus an assurance of certain standards. Each hotel can be independently owned, sharing information and quality control. In the future, a data base may be developed of all hotels in the world (and restaurants and other services, for that matter), which anyone could access from a personal computer, making immediate reservations through pooled telephone lines. Further developments should allow many forms of collaboration and networking to achieve certain advantages of large corporations without losing the identity, flexibility, and risk-taking characteristics of the small business unit.

Conclusion

Small corporations obviously face a disadvantage vis-à-vis the large MNEs, and this disadvantage is growing as markets become more integrated. Large investments are required to develop low-cost sourcing, to nurture an effective international distibution or servicing system, or to run an efficient and integrated network. Small corporations may not only lack the cash, but their management team may be stretched thin by international expansion. Inexperience in global operations and the lack of marketing expertise may jeopardize their operations. Moreover, cross-subsidization and economies of scope across the business units of MNEs may make it more difficult for small corporations to successfully pick a narrow segment of the market requiring a smaller resource commitment and less managerial complexity. Competition in mature markets is often based on cost as much as performance, and small corporations find it much harder than large ones to ride the experience curve to a cost advantage.

Many small companies have grown in the hothouse environment of a protected domestic market and have not adequately recognized the importance of analyzing the market and making the product compatible with the client's needs. Development engineers too often believe that it is enough to make technological breakthroughs, without ascertaining the willingness of the customer to accept the new products.

A small business may encounter difficulties if it tries to expand rapidly in order to retain a dominant share of a growing market. Fortunately, the experience curve is less crucial in a fragmented industry, or where specialization is important.

If a corporation does not become large enough to compete with the world industrial giants at product maturity, it must hope to find a market niche that, because of its limited scope, does not justify a giant's investment in marketing efforts.

Small BUs may be successful in the international arena if they follow the CS2F3 strategy: Customization, Small number of transactions (either because of few large clients or selling a private brand to a large distributor), Superior service, Focus, Fast response, and Flexibility. Those who look at industries rather than at the unique properties of successful strategy might add a fourth F: Fragmented industry. Yet even in the most global of industries, one can find specialty needs that small BUs can cater to.

Small corporations (as distinct from small BUs, which can be part of a large corporation) should attempt to boost exports. The major factor keeping them from foreign markets is the scale required in marketing and after-sale services. Therefore, they may opt for collaborative relations with giants, or with other small corporations through strategic alliances or risk-sharing arrangements, either on their own or with government help.

REFERENCES

Kuno, T., *Strategy and Structure of Japanese Enterprises*, Armonk, N.Y.: Sharpe, 1984.
McClelland, D., "Achievement and Entrepreneurship: A Longitudinal Study," *Journal of Personality and Social Psychology*, Vol. 1, 1965.

PART II
Changing Your Mind-Set, Changing Your Strategy

The globalization of the world market creates substantial opportunities and risks for firms. Managerial action in the face of these opportunities and risks depends on the managerial mind-set. While many U.S.-based multinationals have internalized globalization in their strategy and policies, using international sourcing, offshore financing in various currencies, and so on, most small and midsize firms have not. In the next two chapters, the focus is on the internal process of realization and change that managers of small and midsize American firms must go through to prepare themselves for action.

In Chapter 3, Hekman discusses some possible changes in strategy companies may choose in order to become global competitors and how the changes should be formulated and implemented. In Chapter 4, Caproni, Lenway, and Murtha discuss corporate changes in mind-set and shared meaning, changes that are necessary for the success of the strategy and policy choices prescribed by Hekman.

3

What It Takes to Become a Globally Oriented Corporation

CHRISTINE R. HEKMAN

Globalization of a corporation, whether large or small, requires a restructuring that starts from the deepest levels, the heart of the organization. Executives must rethink the company from a global perspective, beginning with an analysis that involves looking beyond national and cultural boundaries and barriers for resources, people, ideas, capital, and information.

The transition from a local company to a global one starts with basic questions: Who are our customers? What are our products? What do our customers consider to be value? Who are our suppliers, and what are they looking for from the relationship? The new answers must explicitly recognize the global environment.

All analytical and planning processes for complex organizations begin by cutting the task into manageable components. As Milton Friedman pointed out about economics, we divide the world into supply and demand because that is a convenient place to start. So let us approach global restructuring by looking at the traditional organization structure and how it is determined. Miles and Snow give the following description:

> Current theory in the area of strategy, structure, and process is founded largely on the twin concepts of strategic choice and fit. Managers make strategic choices based on their perceptions of the environment and of their

organizations' capabilities. The success of these choices rests on how well competitive strategy matches environmental conditions and whether organizational structure and management processes are properly fitted to strategy. Historically, strategy and structure have evolved together.

Clearly, then, the problem is one of matching strategy, environment, and organizational structures and processes to attain competitive dominance and economic value. The context of this dynamic process is a complex set of interrelated variables, many of which are changing quite rapidly.

Strategy, environment, and organization are themselves composed of essential, characteristic elements. To find a successful match, these elements must be recognized, and the nature of their interrelatedness understood.

How is this problem solved? Organizational theorists have traditionally used the concept of the matrix, balancing the benefits of a functional structure with those of a project or business orientation. As Galbraith puts it,

> The design is specified by the choice among the authority structures; integrating mechanisms such as task forces, teams and so on; and by the formal information system. . . . These design variables help regulate the relative distribution of influence between the product and functional considerations in the firm's operations. . . . There is a choice of integrating devices, authority structure, information system, and influence distribution. The factors that determine choice are diversity of the product line, the rate of change of the product line, interdependencies among subunits, level of technology, presence of economies of scale, and organization size.

I will come back to each of these factors and explore the effects on each of economic globalization and the implications for organizational design, but first I want to explore the idea of organizing the important variables into a matrix.

Applying a simple matrix form to a complex organizational problem is a Procrustean task—one cuts off the pieces that do not fit. But a matrix may help analysis when applied to appropriate subunits, or components, of the aggregate. These components can be divisions, companies, businesses, product lines, or even individuals. In fact, the idea can be extended to produce telescoping matrices, decomposing the problem into subunits and then gathering the reorganized subunits back into the whole corporation.

The new organizational forms cropping up frequently represent structures for relating these basic subunits. Examples include various kinds of strategic alliances, such as joint ventures, subcontracting, outsourcing, licensing, spin-offs, and equity participation, as well as more traditional relationships.

An alternative to the matrix has the general name "dynamic network." This arrangement is a collection of interrelated matrices. (In practice, market mechanisms are used more than plans and controls to hold these systems together.) "Dynamic" suggests flexibility, in this case the capacity for some of the subunits to shift between an autonomy that allows greater responsiveness to the environment and an integration that provides greater corporate efficiency.

Whether we view the organizational form as a matrix or as a dynamic network, we still have to "decompose" the corporation, to identify the essential characteristics of the environment, strategy, and organization, and to understand how to put them together in a way that generates value. Since the matrix form is easier to illustrate and in more general use, that is the approach I will use.

Decomposition into Essential Characteristics

The traditional matrix displays the project across one dimension and the function across another. The "project" may be a corporate division, a company, a business, a product or product line, as well as project in the usual sense of the word. The "function" is a type of activity, such as marketing, production, finance, control, or research responsibilities. Individuals perform functions that contribute to project goals. Most frequently, but not necessarily, projects are operated by teams rather than by a single individual.

For purposes of this analysis, I am replacing the "project" dimension with "environment." This could be done from one of two perspectives. The first is concrete and views the environment as a set of products and markets. The basic transaction is a purchase or sale of a product, and the basic relationship is customer and supplier. In this case, the organizing principles would be the characteristics of the competitive environment: Who are the players? What are their market positions? How is the industry organized?

The second perspective considers the activity itself, not the product, to be the basic unit. Such activities as design, supply, produce, market, distribute, and broker are arrayed along the axis. The organizing principles here would be the characteristics of the market in which the activity or transaction occurs: How is the market structured? Which activities are performed separately and which are bundled? What are the characteristics of market availability and price behavior? This would, of course, be the more effective approach for an analysis of a service business.

Having chosen one of these perspectives to fill the horizontal axis, we must then define the organizational principles for the vertical axis, the types of strategies and organizational forms. There are many variants we could use; one is the topology of Miles and Snow, which organized the strategy/structure dimension into three generic strategies: prospectors, analyzers, and defenders.

Prospectors are market innovators. They are highly autonomous and use flexible, project-oriented organizational forms. Analyzers often follow prospectors, imitating and improving on the initial product design. They tend to use mixed organizational structures, such as the traditional matrix. Defenders hold market share by focusing on rather narrow product lines and by competing on a value or cost basis. These organizations are usually functional in form and contain high levels of specialization.

Those are the two dimensions of our matrix. The cells encompass the personnel, organization, and activities of the company. Our objective is still to match strategy and structure with environmental characteristics in order to achieve the most effective performance. Thus, we return to the question of the environment and to characterization of the environmental elements on which successful performance most depends.

The Traditional Closed Economy or Local Environment

There are a number of ways to organize information about the environment, all of which can be viewed from either internal or external perspectives. An internal perspective addresses the characteristics of the product that have resulted from a strategic review of the environment. The excerpt from Galbraith cited earlier is an example of this. An external perspective focuses more directly on the characteristics of the environment. Burrell and Morgan offer one cut at arranging them:

Stable and certain	Turbulent and unpredictable
Defensive operational goal setting	Proactive creation of learning system
Routine, low discretion roles	Complex, high discretion roles
Economic/instrumental orientation to work	Self-actualizing orientation to work; a central life interest
Mechanistic/bureaucratic	Organic
Authoritarian	Democratic

Since the point is matching the environmental characteristics to strategy and structure, the choice of which to recognize and at what level are crucial to the success of the organization. The Burrell and Morgan scheme represents a single, national environment, assuming a single currency, a unified economy, and one political structure.

The Global Economic Environment

In fact, the global environment is none of those things. It is a world of multiple currencies and currency arrangements, multitudes of local and regional economies, and many separate and influential political entities.

To build these complexities into our analysis, let us start with a distinction between local markets and global markets. A local market is segregated from other local markets. Prices in various markets can, and do, differ from each other significantly. (Prices are considered on an all-in basis. That is, from a single currency perspective, prices are translated by the current foreign exchange rate to yield an effective, all-in, or translated price.) In other words, price depends on geographic location.

Since local markets are, by definition, segregated from other markets to some degree, prices in these markets are determined by local conditions, and are relatively independent of prices in other markets. Hence, there are existing barriers to entry, and competition from other markets is precluded.

Local markets are usually smaller in size than global markets, so there is less scope to gain an advantage through a competitive strategy based on economies of scale. Instead, the "natural" barriers may be used by a particular organization. For example, if the product has culturally important and distinctive qualities, the competitive strategy may be built around brand recognition or design. Other natural barriers include distribution systems, customer and supplier relationship and networks, and organizational or human resource specialties such as are found in service industries.

Local products are closer to the customer, tied to relationships, exhibit cultural differences, are specialized and customized. Sales and service are likely to be significant determinants of competitive success.

Prices and profits are based on higher margins. Customers are frequently insensitive to price, focusing more on other aspects of the product. Producers are therefore relatively free of the need to compete on price and to adjust operations in response to changes in costs.

What do these characteristics of local markets imply for organizations? They are more likely to be prospectors or analysts than defenders. They will focus on marketing, distribution, and design functions, and will be less oriented toward integrating their activities across businesses.

A key point, however, is that arbitrage possibilities exist, at least theoretically, wherever segregated local markets prevent price equalization. Thus, producers for local markets will begin to look to global markets for sourcing in an effort to reduce costs.

In a global market, separate geographical locations are fully integrated. Products and services either flow freely or have the potential to flow freely. Alternatively, the factors of production flow freely, so that prices of assembled products are either very close or identical from market to market. Prices of identical products are everywhere the same regardless of location.

Since the price is set by conditions in the global marketplace, by all participants regardless of geography, culture, and currency, global products must usually compete on the basis of price. Any organization entering these markets must first be confident that costs can be kept sufficiently below this price to insure an adequate profit. For this reason, and because global markets are usually very large, economies of scale in production are the name of the game.

Products marketed globally breed other global products as producers are driven to search for the lowest-cost source of supply. Cost structures, product technologies, and production technologies are more similar across competitors, as all players focus their energies on the management of costs. Product lines are narrower, products are more standardized, and the sales and service component is lower. Products are, or tend to become, more like commodities.

Competitors are more likely to follow the defenders' strategy than the prospectors' or analysts' and to organize accordingly.

By characterizing markets, products, or activities as local or global, a first step in restructuring an organization with global activity in mind is accomplished. From this point, one can go on to distinguish products and businesses according to the type of barrier to entry that is most appropriate. This second step should yield significant gains.

REFERENCES

Burrell, G., and G. Morgan, *Sociological Paradigms and Organizational Analysis: Elements of the Sociology of Corporate Life,* Heineman, 1979.

Galbraith, J.R., "Matrix Organizational Designs," *Business Horizons*, Vol. 14, 1971.

Miles, R.E., and C.C. Snow, "Organizations: New Concepts for New Forms," *California Management Review*, Vol. XXVIII, No. 3, 1986.

Morgan, G., *Images of Organization*, Sage Publications, 1986.

4

Understanding Internationalization: Sense-Making Processes in Multinational Corporations

PAULA J. CAPRIONI
STEFANIE ANN LENWAY
THOMAS P. MURTHA

American prosperity depends, in part, on U.S. firms' abilities to adapt to increasing international competition. Much attention has been paid to the economic, political, technological, strategic, and organizational factors that help or hurt firms as they adjust to global change. International management scholars have built appealing theories of how managers handle the complex tradeoffs among these factors, mostly revolving around the concept that effective organizations fit strategy and structure to environments. But the reality is that what Yves Doz and C. K. Prahalad have called "structural indeterminacy" pervades most successful international organizations. That is, most organizations do not make explicit choices among discrete structural alternatives that trade off factors such as "national responsiveness" and "global integration." Instead, managers examine conflicting environmental demands and organizational objectives and devote increasing attention and resources in responding to them all.

Some theories suggest (and we agree) that structural indeterminacy places a premium on the way managers make sense of their organization and its environment—the organizational meaning system—as a competitive advantage.

As Christopher Bartlett and Sumantra Ghoshal put it after three years in the field studying management activities of multinational corporations (MNCs), "What is critical, then, is not just the structure, but also the mentality of those who constitute the structure. . . . A company's ability to develop transnational organizational capability and management mentality will be the key factor that separates the winners from the mere survivors in the emerging international environment."

C.K. Prahalad and Yves Doz, after six years of research in more than 20 global companies, found much the same thing, observing that in successful multinational organizations "the mindsets of managers, by design, are expected to reflect global and local perspectives. The emerging strategic consensus—local or global—cannot be predicted by the organization chart."

In general, scholars who have looked at the sense-making processes in MNCs focus on (1) the degree to which organizational leaders instill in organization members a common frame of reference and vision that provides direction and enables commitment, communication, coordination, and control; (2) the ways in which organizational knowledge structures and processes serve as a basis for making sense of the environment and formulating strategic decisions; and (3) the ways in which these meaning systems affect the transfer of knowledge, organization learning, and change. These issues may come more self-consciously into play in MNCs than in purely domestic organizations because of the presence of multiple nationalities, ideologies, and cultures. They also help to explain how the geographically discrete, networked subunits that comprise MNCs allow them to remain distinct from the various national environments in which they operate.

Organizational researchers who study sense making share several key assumptions:

- Organizations are systems of meaning.
- Organizational members are boundedly rational.
- Meaning systems are dynamic rather than static.
- Meaning and action are intertwined.
- Sense-making processes in organizations have both functional and dysfunctional consequences.
- Meaning systems and sense-making processes in organizations can and should be managed.

Sense Making and Structure

International management researchers have varied in their prescriptions of structural change as an effective organizational response to increasing international competition. Often the recommended changes have involved matrix solutions that blend the features of several structures. But matrix designs, which attempt to integrate both global product and national market concerns, have often resulted in quagmires of ambiguity, with conflicting lines of authority, communication, and responsibility. Repeated structural changes left organizations reeling from reorganizational whiplash and what Bartlett has called "organizational hangover."

Prescriptions for organizational effectiveness have shifted in recent years toward solutions that avoid restructuring in favor of conserving organizational resources upon which competitive advantage is based, such as individual competence, firm-specific knowledge, and organizational learning capabilities. Bruce Kogut argues that the main strategic advantage of internationalizing a firm lies not in the efficiencies conferred by a more complex and expanded structure, but rather in the enhanced potential for operational flexibility conferred by an international network. The key to the effectiveness of these new, flexible organizations is that they provide their managers with the discretion to compete in a changing environment without constant restructuring.

Discretion to compete, however, does not necessarily translate into capability to do so. Operating a complex and structurally indeterminate organization in a turbulent environment presents a significant intellectual challenge to the individual manager. Bartlett and Ghoshal argue that in order to build a flexible organization, firms must create a "matrix in managers' minds."

Evolution of Multinational Mindsets

Yair Aharoni, in a 1966 study that was perhaps the earliest to focus on management processes in an internationalizing firm, emphasized top managers' "international outlook" as a critical factor in initiating and implementing foreign direct investment.

Three years later, economic historian Charles Kindleberger also implicitly took a sense-making approach to categorize types of international firms. He distinguished the "international corporation" from the "national firm with foreign operations" and the "multinational firm" using criteria that reflected managerial attitudes. The national firm "feels at home in only one country and alien everywhere else." At the other extreme, the international corporation invests its capital according to criteria "free from the myopia that says home investments are automatically risk-free and all foreign investments are risky." Kindleberger wrote,

> The criteria I would pose are two: the company's attitudes toward foreign exchange risk, and toward equalization of profits. The attitudes may be subconscious rather than articulated. The national corporation is usually hedged in foreign exchange, is seldom long in foreign currencies and is

ready to go short when a foreign currency is under attack. It will not take a short position in the currency of the parent company, and does not, in fact recognize that it has an exchange position when it holds net assets denominated in money in that currency. A multinational firm would regard it as breach of good citizenship to go short of a foreign currency. The international firm, on the other hand, is conscious of the exchange risks it takes in any currency, including that of the parent country.

The influence of this element of organizational symbolism in Kindleberger's thought may be reflected seventeen years later, in Donald Lessard's metaphor of currency-colored eyeglasses that "distort traditional measures of current and long-term profitability, creating illusions that depend on the currency in which alternatives are weighed and a manager's performance is judged." In MNCs, what managers see depends on the representation of value adopted within the organization.

Howard V. Perlmutter, a psychologist, was the first to systematically frame the core dialectic of international management—the reconciliation of country-level environmental demands and opportunities to the corporation's global systemic need for efficiency—in terms of specific types of knowledge structures. Knowledge structures are also called frames of reference or world views. They are implicit theories used to bring meaning to patterns of action within organizations and to make connections between organizations and their environments. James Walsh points out that although knowledge structures embody causal beliefs that guide action, they do not necessarily reflect empirically verifiable causal relationships.

After conducting interviews in a number of multinational corporations, Perlmutter described three "primary attitudes" underlying corporate strategy: ethnocentric, polycentric, and geocentric orientations. These fit neatly onto Kindleberger's organizational map (see Figure 4.1).

In head offices where ethnocentric attitudes prevail, home nationals believe themselves to be superior to, more trustworthy, and more reliable than foreign nationals either in headquarters or subsidiaries. Ethnocentric firms tend to centralize authority in headquarters, to use home-country standards to evaluate performance, to have heavy information flows between head office and affiliates, and to recruit exclusively home-country nationals for key positions.

In firms where polycentric attitudes hold sway, top executives assume that "host-country cultures are different and that foreigners are difficult to understand." Such firms tend to decentralize authority, to evaluate performance using local standards, to engage in relatively little headquarters-subsidiary or subsidiary-subsidiary communication, and to develop local nationals for key positions in their own country.

In firms with geocentric orientations, subsidiaries act interdependently as "parts of the whole whose focus is on worldwide as well as local objectives, each part making its unique contribution with its

Porter (1986)	Prahalad & Doz (1987)	Hedlund (1986, 1990)	Bartlett & Ghoshal (1989)	Kindleberger (1969)	Perlmutter (1969)
Industry	Firm Strategy	Firm Organization	Firm Organization	Managerial Attitudes	Managers' Cognitive Orientations
Simple Global	Global Integration	Hierarchy	Global	National Firm with International Operations	Ethnocentric
Multidomestic	National Responsiveness	Hierarchy	Multinational	Multinational	Polycentric
Complex Global	Multifocal	Heterarchy	Transnational	International	Geocentric

Figure 4.1 Taxonomies of international strategy and organization.

unique competence." Performance evaluation rewards actions that enhance the global standing of the firm and discourages actions that enhance local performance at the expense of global performance. Communication flows take place along intersubsidiary and headquarters-subsidiary lines. The best-qualified person is sought for any given position, without regard to the position's location or the ethnicity of the job candidate.

Mind over Matrix

These three managerial mindsets represent developmental stages in the evolution of global business in which MNCs with geocentric orientations have attained the highest form. Neither Perlmutter's nor Kindleberger's taxonomy has a strong empirical base, but both are intuitively appealing. Many later studies have expanded on these ideas and have provided evidence to support them (see Figure 4.1).

Contemporary theories of international management process, as represented by these studies, do not envision continual structural transformations of organizations as they evolve from local responsiveness toward global orientations. Instead, the studies specify steps to implement what Vladimir Pucik calls a "global matrix culture." Prahalad and Doz define this as a "decision-making culture where multiple and often conflicting points of view are explicitly examined."

To emphasize the need for a balance among the cognitive orientations of product, geographic, and functional management, Bartlett and Ghoshal identified characteristics of highly evolved "transnational" firms, as distinct from country- or product-centered organizational forms. Transnationals simultaneously pursue global competitiveness, national responsiveness, and intracorporate transfer of innovations. Like Prahalad and Doz, Bartlett and Ghoshal counsel against structural change as a tactic for overcoming an "administrative heritage" that inhibits firm internationalization. Instead, they suggest that the transnational organization protect its existing knowledge base while cultivating a new managerial vision that will lead to new capabilities.

Both pairs of authors caution MNCs to avoid creating global vision at the expense of diversity of perspectives. Organizations ensure against the loss of diversity and a narrowing of vision by providing geographic managers, product division managers, and corporate staff functional managers with legitimacy, influence, and resource access to enable them to advance their viewpoints. The organization must then manage relationships among these groups to resolve the tensions that arise from their respective orientations toward efficiency, responsiveness, and learning. As Bartlett and Ghoshal put it, organizational flexibility relies on a "managerial mentality throughout the company that co-opts individual employees into sharing the corporate vision," creating "a matrix in the mind of managers." Evolution toward transnationalism requires changes in individual attitudes and mentalities, followed by changes in interpersonal relationships and processess, and finally, changes in formal structures and responsibilities.

Gunnar Hedlund argues that, in contrast to traditional notions of hierarchy in business organizations, the structure of the transnational is in reality a "heterarchy." This description acknowledges that modern organizations widely distribute the power to allocate resources, to establish meaning, to lead innovation, and so on. Organizational units that act as primary global decision-makers in one area may completely subordinate themselves in others. Factors such as geographic location, market characteristics, horizontal information flows, technical expertise, and fast-paced changes in business conditions may often create business situations where organization members' discretion and their hierarchical positions do not coincide.

Heterarchy is a way of relating organizational components along dimensions of knowledge and action as well as authority. In order to maintain cohesion in heterarchies, Hedlund writes, "shared objectives and knowledge, and a common organizational culture and symbolism are important mechanisms. Investments in communication systems, rotation of personnel, a bias for internal promotion, and other human resource management strategies become increasingly important." The global heterarchy's competitive advantage over time is in its organizing processes, in a form that Hedlund, recalling Michael Polanyi, calls "social tacit knowledge."

Propositions and Conclusions

The theories discussed here lead to several propositions that we believe could be usefully explored in future studies.

The first proposition focuses on the symbolic aspect of sense making and relies on the perspective of Clayton Alderfer in his work with K. K. Smith. We expect that members at the same level of the organizational hierarchy, whether factory workers, middle managers, or executives, regardless of the organization to which they belong, will tend to share similar views of internationalization. Within the psychological and physical boundaries of hierarchical group memberships, members would learn a common language of internationalization and a framework that would guide their interpretations and responses to events. Hence:

Proposition 1: Members at different levels of the organization hierarchy in MNCs will have different interpretations of, and experiences with, "internationalization."

Other propositions focus on knowledge structures. We expect the cognitive complexity of knowledge structures to vary with the international strategy and organization of the MNC. Borrowing from Bartunek, Gordon, and Weathersby, and the work of James Walsh, we suggest that cognitive complexity can be measured in two dimensions: differentiation, or the ability of the organization to make distinctions in the nature of product and functional activities on the basis of geographic context, and integration, which is the ability of the firm to unify the product and functional knowledge structures with each other and across geographic areas in the actions undertaken by the firm. Higher levels of both differentiation and integration are associated with higher levels of organizational effectiveness.

Figure 4.1 draws parallels among the attributes of MNCs as described by several leading scholars. In each case, the distinctions rely on differences with respect to the level of interdependence between the headquarters and subsidiaries and among subsidiaries. Further, these distinctions result from the evolution from a dominant headquarters, to relatively autonomous and self-sufficient subsidiaries, to a structure in which there is a high degree of interdependence. We would also expect an evolution to a higher level of cognitive complexity.

The strong headquarters control in ethnocentric firms results in relatively undifferentiated knowledge structures, even across geographic areas. Ethnocentric firms, which Perlmutter defines in part as "using exactly the same criteria to evaluate investment projects" both at home and abroad, are not likely to take into account the implications for the variation in product and functional concerns of operating in a geographic location outside the home country. The high level of headquarters control also makes it unlikely that knowledge structures from the subsidiaries are integrated into those of headquarters. (To the extent that knowledge structures found in subsidiaries resemble those of the parent, we expect that the similarity results from the influence of headquarters rather than the integration of the subsidiary perspective into a firm-wide knowledge structure.) Thus:

Proposition 2: Firms with ethnocentric attributes are likely to have relatively undifferentiated knowledge structures that are not integrated across the international operations of the firm.

In contrast, as Perlmutter writes, polycentric firms "begin with the assumption that host-country cultures are different and that foreigners are difficult to understand." In an effort to make the subsidiary look and act as much as possible like a local firm, headquarters has to accept a high degree of differentiation in the knowledge structures used in accomplishing the objectives of the firm across geographic locations. However, the low degree of information flow both between headquarters and subsidiaries and among subsidiaries suggests that these knowledge structures are not well integrated. Therefore:

Proposition 3: Firms with polycentric attributes are likely to have relatively differentiated knowledge structures that are not integrated across the international operations of the firm.

In geocentric firms, Perlmutter characterized subsidiaries as "neither satellites nor independent city states, but parts of a whole whose focus is on worldwide objectives as well as local objectives, each part making its unique contribution with its unique competence." To determine each subsidiary's unique contribution involves a high level of differentiation across geographic locations. To achieve a high level of interdependence involves both a high level of integration among the knowledge structures of individual subsidiaries and headquarters as well as a high level of integration among the geographic, product, and functional subgroups within the firm. On this basis we propose:

Proposition 4: Firms with geocentric attributes will have a high level of differentiation in knowledge structures that are integrated across subsidiaries.

Our final proposition addresses the question of changes in knowledge structures. The above "drama in three acts," as Perlmutter describes it, suggests that firms first experience an increase in the differentiation of their knowledge structures in their transition from an ethnocentric to a polycentric cognitive orientation. Integration comes later with the transition to geocentrism. Thus, we suggest:

Proposition 5: The ability of multinationals to integrate across complex knowledge structures comes only after they develop increasingly more differentiated knowledge structures.

Propositions such as these challenge us conceptually, promise to broaden our knowledge of sense-making processes in MNCs, and ultimately may result in new prescriptions for enhancing organizational survival and success. Framing multinational corporations as interpretive systems helps researchers and practitioners alike understand why organizations embrace, resist, or muddle through internationalization. Only the adjustment of individuals, work groups, and business organizations to increasing internationalization and economic openness will permit country-level structural adjustment. It is in this context that we hope to understand internationalization: from the perspective that thinking individuals ultimately do—or do not do—the internationalizing.

REFERENCES

Aharoni, Y., *The Foreign Investment Decision Process*, Division of Research, Graduate School of Business, Harvard University, 1966.

Alderfer, C.P., and K.K. Smith, "Studying Intergroup Relations Embedded in Organizations," *Administrative Science Quarterly*, Vol. 27, 1982.

Bartenuk, J.M., J.R. Gordon, and R.P. Weathersby, "Developing a 'Complicated' Understanding in Administrators," *Academy of Management Review*, Vol. 8, 1983.

Bartlett, C., "MNCs: Get Off the Reorganization Merry-Go-Round," *Harvard Business Review*, Mar.-Apr. 1983.

Bartlett, C.A., and S. Ghoshal, *Managing Across Borders: The Transnational Solution*, Harvard University Press, 1989.

Doz, Y., and C.K. Prahalad, "Managing MNCs: A Search for a New Paradigm," *Strategic Management Journal*, in press.

Hedlund, G., "The Hypermodern MNC: A Heterarchy?" *Human Resource Management*, Vol. 25, No. 1, 1986.

———, "Assumptions of Hierarchy and Heterarchy: With Application to the Management of the Multinational Corporation," Stockholm School of Economics Working Paper 90/4, May 1990.

Kindleberger, C., *American Business Abroad: Six Lectures on Direct Investment*, Yale University Press, 1969.

Kogut, B., "Designing Global Strategy: Profiting from Operational Flexibility," *Sloan Management Review,* Vol. 26, No. 5, 1985.

Lessard, D., "Finance and Global Competition: Exploiting Financial Scope and Coping With Volatile Exchange Rates," *Competition in Global Industries* (M. Porter, ed.), Harvard Business School Press, 1986.

Perlmutter, H.V., "The Tortuous Evolution of the Multinational Corporation," *Columbia Journal of World Business*, Jan.-Feb. 1969.

Polanyi, M., *Personal Knowledge*, University of Chicago Press, 1958.

Prahalad, C.K., and Y.L. Doz, *The Multinational Mission: Balancing Local Demands and Global Vision*, Free Press, 1987.

Pucik, V., "The International Management of Human Resources," *Strategic Human Resource Management* (C.J. Fombrun, N.M. Tichy, and M.A. DeVanna, eds.), John Wiley and Sons, 1984.

Walsh, J., "Knowledge Structures and the Management of Organizations: A Research Review and Agenda," Pers. Commun., 1990.

PART III
The Environment of Global Markets

Proper mind-set and strategy are necessary but not sufficient conditions for becoming internationally competitive. The global business environment, described in this section, has substantial effects on a firm's ability to compete.

As the first three chapters in this section testify, the global environment is complex and rapidly changing. In Chapter 5, Weinstein explains why world financial markets are integrated and how this integration affects corporate financial decisions. He argues that every firm—knowingly or not—operates in an efficient, integrated world financial system.

Others argue, however, that international markets are separated by different cultures, conventions, laws, and regulations. In Chapter 6, Elnathan and Arnold provide ample evidence of different national practices in recording and evaluating financial data. They conclude that harmonization is needed because, in its absence, the different national accounting practices constitute a barrier to global integration by preventing firms from using a single accounting and reporting model. Because of their limited resources, small firms are likely to be affected more than large firms.

Trade laws are also barriers to global integration, in the United States and elsewhere. Rugman and Gestrin focus in Chapter 7 on the market-distorting effects of U.S. trade laws, but examples of such national barriers to trade flows are pervasive.

To operate successfully in global markets, small and midsize firms need the ability to communicate across cultures. This is true whether they try to "go it alone" or form cross-national alliances. Intercultural communication is the subject of Chapter 8, in which Reardon and Spekman discuss some practicalities of interfirm negotiation, the first step in those alliances.

5

The Accessibility of International Financial Markets

MARK WEINSTEIN

My father once had a small business that involved importing and distributing ceramic tile. His purchase price was in yen, while he sold in dollars. After the international money market (IMM) opened, I suggested that he consider hedging his yen exposure. He declined, stating that he did not choose to speculate on a foreign currency. Of course, by not hedging he was speculating, but it took some time for him to see that. In the same way, it has taken time for farmers in Illinois to realize that, even if they sell their grain in the domestic market, what happens overseas plays a major role in the transaction. There is a world market for grain, and even those who do not participate in it directly are affected because the world market determines prices.

The international integration of capital markets is best viewed like the punch of Muhammad Ali: You can run, but you can't hide. In effect, every investor is an international investor. Every issuing firm is an international issuer. World capital market risks are reflected in the price of U.S. securities, even if those particular firms are primarily domestic. And even if there is little or no cross-listing of securities between the major stock exchanges of the world, the risk/return tradeoff will reflect exposure to foreign as well as domestic risks. The smallest investor and the smallest issuer are both affected by international risk.

Before discussing several reasons why this is the case, I want to

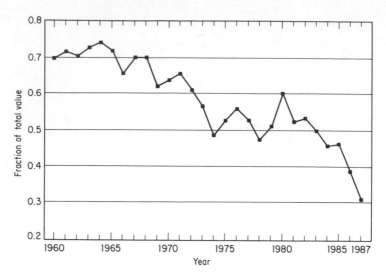

Figure 5.1 Market value of NYSE as a fraction of NYSE + London + Tokyo (annual data, 1960–1987).

provide a little background information. As a share of global equity values, the New York Stock Exchange is declining in importance. Figure 5.1 presents annual observations of the dollar value of all listed securities on the world's three largest stock exchanges, London, New York, and Tokyo, from 1960 to 1991. It is clear that the United States has declined in *relative* importance. This was to be expected—indeed, if it had not occurred, we would have to deem the Marshall Plan and all the postwar reconstruction aid provided to both Europe and Japan to have been wasted.

The relative diminution of the U.S. share of the world securities markets is not limited to equities. Consider financial futures contracts—an American invention. Nevertheless, from 1980 to 1990, the U.S. share of trading volume in financial futures contracts declined from 100 percent to 63 percent. This trend can be expected to continue.

Moreover, there is increasing evidence of international competition in capital markets. For example, the recent move by the NYSE to introduce after-hours trading of securities baskets is driven by an attempt to recapture the substantial basket-trading business that has fled New York for London because the trading mechanisms are more efficient there.

These are examples of three main facts that govern world capital markets: First, the U.S. share of global securities trading is declining; second, innovations in securities design and trading are quickly copied; and third, there is increasing competition among securities exchanges for the worldwide trading volume that the exchanges need to survive.

This competition shows up in a number of ways—not the least of which is the increasing ability of domestic firms to tap foreign capital markets. The Eurodollar debt market, which initially arose because of U.S. capital controls, has grown to become a viable source of financing for large and even not-so-large U.S. borrowers, from IBM to the now-infamous American Continental Corporation, former home of Charles Keating. Japan, which until recently had no domestic corporate bond market to speak of, now has a thriving one.

Because there are many opportunities for international arbitrage by both investors and issuers, I believe it makes more sense to think in terms of a single world capital market with a single set of risks and risk/return tradeoffs determining securities prices than to think of a myriad of separate national markets. This arbitrage, mainly (though not completely) carried out by large issuers and purchasers, acts to transmit international risks into the domestic capital markets so that even purely domestic firms are priced according to "world" pricing. Therefore, all investors face the same risk/return tradeoff, whether or not they choose to invest internationally. And issuers, even if they only issue in the domestic markets—indeed, even if they only borrow from a bank—face the same costs of funds that they would face internationally.

Risk and Price

To understand this, it is important to consider how modern finance views securities pricing and risk. The many pricing models all share a common framework, in which the expected return on a security is made up of two components. First, any risky security must offer the possibility of a return at least equal to the return on a riskless asset, simply to compensate investors for the time value of tying up their money. Second, over and above this, the expected return must include a risk premium to compensate investors for bearing risk that could have been avoided. Given the (assumed) competitive nature of capital markets, the risk premium is equal to a constant price of risk (per unit of risk) multiplied by a risk exposure.

Figure 5.2 presents an example of how this works in the Sharpe Capital Asset Pricing Model. The various models differ in the way that risk is measured, but for our purposes we will measure risk (and this is not without some controversy) by exposure to unanticipated changes in GNP, which translates into the return on the market portfolio. Loosely speaking, this is the "beta" for which William Sharpe shared the 1991 Nobel Prize for economics. The real question then is, "The return on *whose* market portfolio?" For example, if the world consisted of a separate set of islands, none of which had any trade or commerce with another, the appropriate market portfolio to use for risk measurement

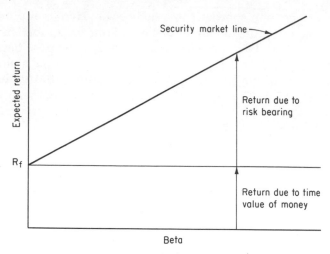

Figure 5.2 The slope of the security market line depends upon risk preferences and the riskiness of the market portfolio.

would be the *domestic* one. At the other extreme, if all capital, labor, and product markets were fully integrated so that there was, in effect, a single country in the world (just as we do not view the fifty states as fifty separate countries), the appropriate GNP would be the *world* market portfolio. The truth lies in between. The question becomes one of whether the first or second image better approximates reality.

One more point along this line: A U.S. firm that does a major portion of its business in, say, the United Kingdom, has cash flows (and when cash flows are capitalized at the appropriate risk-adjusted discount rate, they are the value of the firm) that are sensitive to what happens in the United Kingdom. We might say this firm has a high beta with respect to this risk. A U.S. firm that does no direct business with the United Kingdom would have a low beta with respect to this risk. In that sense, the more international a firm is in its operations, the more it needs to pay attention to the world at large. However, if capital markets are integrated, then the market price of risk (the slope of the security market line) is affected not only by the risk preferences and wealth of domestic investors, but also by the risk preferences and wealth of foreign investors. Indeed, as the United States shrinks in proportion to the rest of the world, we would expect that, more and more, the price of risk in the U.S. capital markets is determined by non-U.S. investors. This is neither good nor bad—any more than it is good or bad that the price of soybeans is determined in the world soybean market. The capital market is simply the market for risk allocation, just as the soybean market is the market for soybean allocation.

Debt or Equity or What?

Back to our main theme. Consider the implications for a large, well-known American firm that has to raise money. In finance, we normally think in terms of a choice between debt and equity. But in today's world, the possibilities are almost endless: Debt or equity? Dollar or Eurodollar or yen or sterling?

Consider, too, our simple domestic (U.S.) investor who never wanted to hear of foreign risks (he has enough trouble getting things straight at home). Clearly, if the company he invests in has significant foreign operations, he is exposed to the risk associated with the foreign economies. This is not necessarily bad. For years Ford was performing dismally in the United States and depending upon its strong European operations for survival. However—and this is the point—even if the firm does not invest abroad, but only raises funds abroad, our friend is going to discover that what goes on overseas affects his wealth. For illustration, hold the value of the firm constant, and imagine that the firm issues equity domestically, but has a single foreign debt issue. Since the value of the firm is fixed, variation in the value of the debt must cause equal and offsetting variation in the value of the firm's equity. This means that a change in the compensation demanded by foreign investors for bearing the default risk associated with the debt issue will change the value of the debt—and hence the value of the equity.

Now let us suppose that the slope of the security market line (the price of risk) differs significantly between two markets (after adjusting for liquidity and tax effects). Clearly, the firm will issue securities where it can get the highest price—that is, where the compensation that must be offered to investors for risk-bearing is lowest. If there are enough large issuers of securities who can choose where to issue their securities, they will bring about equality of market prices for risk bearing. Thus, not only will holders of securities issued by firms with foreign securities discover that nondomestic risks affect their expected return, but as a result of arbitrage on the supply side, so will investors in firms that appear to have no foreign operations whatsoever. Of course, for those firms, the betas with respect to foreign risks may be low. They will nevertheless be present. Arbitrage on the part of issuers thus becomes a driving force for "world" rather than "domestic" pricing.

Issuers of securities are not the only ones who engage in international securities markets arbitrage. The same arbitrage is clearly possible for large investors, such as the major investment firms that arbitrage internationally traded securities between New York and London. Many, if not most, large pension plans have international equity and debt portions of their portfolios. Individual investors can select from a myriad of mutual funds that invest in foreign securities. It is even possible to invest in individual foreign securities, through the American Depositary Receipts (ADRs) that trade in the United States. Moreover, given that a number of U.S. securities firms do business in Japan and Europe, one could open an account with an overseas branch of the firm. We still do not have integrated clearing mechanisms in stocks (the futures markets are more innovative here), but any investor who desires exposure to foreign risks can achieve it fairly easily.

Those investors who have chosen to diversify their portfolios internationally will view the purchase of any security in terms of its expected return and its beta with respect to the world market portfolio. If there are enough of them, or if they have enough money (and remember that price is determined by the marginal investor), they will ensure that even securities that do not trade abroad are priced as though they did— because if they are not, these investors have an arbitrage opportunity.

Moreover, it is not always clear what a foreign security is. Take Sony as an example. In a very real sense, Sony is not a Japanese corporation, but rather an American one. Its cash flows are more dependent on sales in the United States than in Japan, and it has a considerable investment here. The information that moves the stock is information from the U.S., not the Japanese, market. Thus Sony would have a reasonably high beta with respect to the U.S. market.

International arbitrage has a third dimension, besides issuers and investors. Derivative securities also play a role. Some derivatives, like the Nikkei Index puts, allow players to speculate in a portfolio of foreign securities. Others are a little more interesting. For example, new uses of "swaps" enable foreign investors in effect to purchase the cash flows associated with securities that have legally restricted ownership. A U.S. investor might want to purchase stock in a Swedish company, whose shares must be owned by a Swede. A broker finds a Swedish national to purchase the stock. The Swede then swaps the cash flows (which the U.S. investor acquires) for London InterBank Offering Rate (LIBOR) plus a risk premium.

A U.S. investment banking firm engaged in a similar swap to avoid restrictions on short selling in Tokyo. Having written some Nikkei puts, the firm wanted to hedge its risk exposure. It did so by purchasing a portfolio of Japanese stocks and swapping the cash flows for LIBOR plus a risk premium. Thus, the firm maintained ownership of the portfolio without bearing the risks associated with the Tokyo market. To hedge the risk associated with the Nikkei put position, then, it can simply sell some of this portfolio—that is, rather than physically going short, it reduces its long position. Note, however, that even though legally the firm is long in the Japanese market (it does have title to the securities), from a risk-bearing point of view it is neither long nor short, because it has swapped all of the cash flows.

These innovations make it easier to bring world pricing to the domestic market. And every mechanism that brings world pricing to the U.S. market also takes it to any of the larger foreign markets.

So what is the bottom line? XYZ, a U.S. firm, will be priced in a manner consistent with its beta in respect to both the U.S. and Tokyo exchanges. Investors cannot escape exposure to "foreign" risk. Even if they choose securities whose beta with respect to London and Tokyo is zero, the slope of the risk/return tradeoffs is determined in the world securities market in which British and Japanese investors operate and hence depends on the risk preferences and wealth of foreign investors.

In sum, the international effects of asset pricing cannot be avoided.

6

Accounting Aspects of Globalizing American Firms

DAN ELNATHAN
JERRY L. ARNOLD

When American firms consider a strategic plan for globalization, the accounting issues are all too frequently addressed as an afterthought. An approach that integrates accounting from the beginning, however, enhances the likelihood of success and minimizes the chance of a suboptimal accounting system. In most instances, American firms must adapt to the environment in the host country; effecting change in another country's accounting system is likely to be politically sensitive and to take a long time, if it happens at all.

Having made the decision to "go international," the company must also understand the impact on its own accounting system. There will be a direct impact because of unique transactions, exposure to fluctuations in foreign currency exchange rates, hedging, and adjustment of performance evaluation measures. There will be an indirect effect from the accounting environment in the host country and its national accounting system.

The accounting environment is defined as the broad characteristics of recording and reporting information in the country and society in which the national accounting system is developed. A national accounting system, then, is the institutional setting in which accounting standards and practices are developed, used, and enforced. This system in-

46

cludes regulators (Securities and Exchange Commission in the United States), standard setters (Financial Accounting Standards Board in the United States), the accounting profession (American Institute of Certified Public Accountants and accounting firms), preparers, and users (equity and debt investors, analysts, and stock exchanges). It is influenced by and is a reflection of the environment, which includes economic, educational, legal, political, and sociocultural factors.

To operate effectively in foreign countries, American firms must be aware of the diversity and dynamics of local environments. They should understand the reasons for such diversity and its impact on a wide range of accounting issues, such as financial accounting standards, regulation, and compliance; audit standards and techniques; management accounting practices, control systems, and performance measures; and national taxation policy and tax accounting.

The Accounting Environment

Accounting is the language of business, and it develops like any other language as an integral part of the environment. This means that the way one measures, records, or reports a similar transaction in different countries changes with the surroundings. For example, land is recorded under the U.S. Generally Accepted Accounting Principles (GAAP) as a fixed, nondepreciable asset. In Hong Kong, however, land leasehold is a depreciable asset, terminating in 1997, while in the former Soviet Union, land was owned only by the government and did not show up on any individual enterprise balance sheet.

Each of the five major groups of environmental characteristics— economic, educational, legal, political, and sociocultural—can serve as a catalyst or constraint for the firm's ability to operate efficiently.

A country's stage of economic development and basic economic orientation are major factors influencing accounting development and practice. At extremely low levels of economic development, for example, there is little economic activity and therefore little financial, tax, or managerial accounting. As economic activity and the size of business enterprises increase (usually in tandem), the complexity of the transactions that the accounting system has to measure, record, and report also increases. Accounting issues pertaining to software development are not relevant in Third World agricultural economies, and procedures for mergers and acquisitions are not required in economies dominated by sole proprietorships and government-owned corporations.

The relevant educational characteristics include the degree of literacy (including mathematical literacy), the percentage of people with formal schooling (and the level achieved), and the orientation (such as religious or scientific) and match (of output to needs) of the educational system. For example, a high level of education is a necessary condition for a skilled work force. The degree of literacy influences the amount of time a firm should invest in designing external and internal accounting systems and what it should expect of its employees, local business contacts, and government agencies. Where accounting is taught in high schools, and where advanced accounting degrees are offered, the functions of budgeting, control, and auditing will be relatively advanced. There will be a higher level of accounting literacy and a greater demand for disclosure requirements.

The legal environment is frequently classified as either a Code or a Common Law environment. In many countries the laws—particularly tax laws—are the primary cause of accounting activity. The accounting rules and practices are explicitly included in laws, often called Companies' Acts, which also contain other directives and regulations concerning business activities. Even where tax is not the only reason for accounting, tax laws frequently specify the procedures to be used for tax purposes.

Personal privacy protection laws in most Western European countries restrict the electronic transmission of payroll and human resources information from the subsidiary to the home office of the multinational corporation (MNC). Other restrictions on transborder data flow include physical monitoring of data transmissions, import control on hardware and software, or requirements to use locally produced hardware and software. A study by S. Ewer found that such legal restrictions adversely affect the corporate accounting control systems of U.S.-based MNCs. For example, the accounting system's flexibility and the timeliness of the reports are impaired.

Political factors also influence accounting systems and practices. In socialist countries, the government sees it as politically expedient and desirable to require from companies certain information about the social impact of various activities. For similar reasons, developing countries may require reports from companies regarding the impact of their planned operations on the balance of payments before approving an investment. Changes in political orientation can bring about new accounting rules through new laws. In extreme cases, when firms are nationalized, the accounting records serve as the basis for the establishment of the fair market value the owners would expect to receive.

Among the most important sociocultural factors are the degree of conservatism, secrecy, fatalism, materialism, norms of ethical behavior, and the loyalty to society and family. Certain cultural characteristics, such as the tendency to avoid contact with strangers, may result in poor communication between an expatriate manager and local employees. Incentive schemes that may be acceptable in the home country (such as bonus plans in the United States) may not work well in a foreign country where nonmonetary rewards, such as a title or job security, might be the desired form of recognition.

In a study of IBM employees in sixty-three countries, Greet Hofstede developed a map based on cultural measures. Two of those measures, power distance (the ability to accept unequal power distribution in the organization) and uncertainty avoidance (the level of anxiety in the face of uncertainty) are particularly relevant for the analysis of national accounting systems. In countries with high uncertainty avoidance, for example, a highly structured accounting system would be preferred by employees. In a low power-distance environment, however, a rigid reporting and control system would not work. The most important lesson from Hofstede's analysis is that firms should evaluate the cultural proximity between their home environment and the new environment before deciding which accounting, reporting, and control systems to implement.

Characteristics of Accounting Systems

We defined an accounting system as the institutional setting in which accounting standards and practices are developed, used, and enforced. Describing system characteristics entails answering questions such as:

- Who sets the accounting standards?
- Toward what primary group is the system oriented?
- Who enforces the standards and through what means?
- How advanced is the profession?
- How significant is the audit function?
- What types of reports and other documents are required?

In the United States, a federal regulator (Securities and Exchange Commission) delegates authority, with oversight, to a private-sector standard setter (Financial Accounting Standards Board, an independent body of accountants). The American Institute of Certified Public Accountants (AICPA) sets generally accepted auditing standards (GAAS), also with SEC oversight, and requires its members to comply with both GAAP and GAAS. The SEC has enforcement power granted by Congress in the 1934 Securities Exchange Act, which it makes use of when necessary.

Accounting information is used to make investment decisions in a market economy. Debt and equity investors, securities analysts, and stock exchanges are prime users. The SEC requires annual audits and financial reports from companies whose stock is listed on exchanges, or that have more than 500 shareholders and more than $5 million in assets. Many smaller U.S. companies have annual audited financial statements prepared at the request of banks or other creditors, corporate boards of directors, and management.

In contrast to the American system, the accounting systems of Germany and Japan are tax oriented. The results of operations are accepted for tax purposes only if they are also reported in the financial statements. The French system is macroeconomic: A uniform set of accounts is kept by all state-owned companies and most public firms in order to provide standard information to the central decision-making agencies charged with managing a planned economy.

Yet another approach is taken in the Netherlands, where standard setting is a joint effort of many groups, including labor and academia. Accounting disputes are resolved in a singular institution—an Accounting Court. There the combined inputs of a Code legal system, a democratic, tolerant, and open society, and a capitalist market economy influence accounting standards. This accounting system is unique among all developed countries in its flexibility and theoretical-economic orientation.

In the Soviet Union and other communist systems, the chief bookkeeper is the link to the state government, and thus the position ranks high in the corporate structure, with responsibilities and authority over managerial decisions.

Around the World of Accounting Practices

The numbers of diverse practices and combinations thereof preclude our describing them all. However, we can show how the environmental and system fundamentals drive the diversity and illustrate why American firms with foreign linkages must understand the background for such practices.

Many experienced managers develop a sense for what their reported earnings will be, given the details of the operation. However, when these operations are conducted abroad and reported under foreign accounting standards, those expectations may prove wrong. A study by Wygal, Stout, and Volpi compared the reported earnings for four hypothetical firms operating in the United States, United Kingdom, Australia, and Germany. The four were given identical economic transactions during the reporting period, but the operating results were vastly different because of the accounting practices involved. The reported net income for the American firm was 15 percent of the Australian and the British net profit, and three times greater than the German. Conducting this kind of exercise before starting foreign operations can prove useful in giving management a more realistic picture of expected results.

Auditing provides another example of differing standards. As a company expands overseas, it relies more on the accuracy of the reported results, as verified by internal and external auditors. However, American firms should be careful of their assumptions about foreign audit practices and ethical norms. Karnes, Sterner, Welker, and Wu asked whether public accountants' national culture affects their perception of unethical business practices, comparing accountants from a highly individualistic society, the United States, and a highly collectivist society, Taiwan. They discovered that American accountants appeared to focus on the legal ramifications of the unethical business practices, a rational response to the individualistic and litigious society in which they live. Taiwanese accountants, on the other hand, seemed to differentiate among unethical business practices on the basis of the in-group (family, business, nation) affected and to balance the magnitude of the benefits against the perceived harm that could arise from the ethical breach.

In some cases the measurement of revenues and costs is so different that it is difficult to generate comparable operating results. Land and natural resources in the former Soviet Union do not belong to any single enterprise and therefore are not recorded on balance sheets. The political-economic environment that gave rise to the communist accounting system did not recognize economic costs for the use of capital, land, and natural resources. Depletion, rent, and interest expense were viewed as exploitative capitalistic practices and were not charged to the firm. We expect that accounting standards will soon begin to reflect the changes in Russian society. Indeed, several Western accountants have been commissioned by the United Nations to lead the accounting revolution in the former Soviet Union by educating Russian accountants in the practices required in a market economy.

High inflation for long periods distorts values and creates problems in budgeting, tracking results, and evaluating performance. Israel, for one, has taken steps to create appropriate accounting standards. Financial results in that country are adjusted to reflect General Purchase Power (GPP) fluctuations, and the tax law recognizes inflation adjustments to capital assets. Where inflation accounting is required or allowed, the financial statements of subsidiaries cannot be combined with parent statements without distortion. Similarly, they cannot be compared without adjustment to reports from other foreign subsidiaries in order to evaluate relative subsidiary and manager performance.

Accounting for Alternative Forms of Globalization

The various forms of globalization—export/import, foreign branch and subsidiary operations, and joint ventures—have different accounting implications because of different standards, regulations, and treatments that apply. Whichever form is chosen, one of the most complex and controversial issues the firm will face is accounting for foreign currency translations. Companies with significant operations abroad cannot prepare consolidated statements unless all accounts are expressed in terms of a single currency. This is traditionally the reporting currency of the parent company, which may not be the currency of the parent's home country. For example, some non-American companies use the U.S. dollar as their reporting currency because most of their business activity is conducted in dollars. Some also have their shares traded on American stock exchanges, adding an incentive to carry out all accounting-system operations in accordance with U.S. GAAP, as well as their local GAAP. There are also specific problems, such as the assignment of the foreign currency translation to the subsidiary manager. In the process operating results may be overwhelmed, and the impact of non-currency related performance may be obscured.

But as described earlier, the differences go beyond translation. Different practices for alternative forms of globalization include accounting for consolidated entities, requirements for segment reporting, and alternative asset valuation approaches, just to name a few.

Export/Import Transactions

Export/import transactions are typically the first experiences in cross-border operations. Because financial statements cannot be prepared from accounts that are expressed in various currencies, if the firm's exports or imports are invoiced in foreign currency units, the transactions must be translated to the domestic currency before being entered in the books. Under U.S. accounting standards, the company has to measure and record a transaction on the date it occurs, using the exchange rate in effect on that date. On each balance sheet date, recorded balances for accounts receivable and payable denominated in foreign currency must be adjusted to reflect the current exchange rate. Transaction gains or losses are reflected in income in the period in which the exchange rate changes.

The implications are straightforward. While the transaction that gave rise to the accounting entry may not have been closed by the end of the reporting period, the accounting standards require a periodic recognition of the exchange rate fluctuation on the income statement. The practice is called the Two-Transaction approach, referring to the effective separation of the sale transaction and the subsequent "financing" decision.

Another problem of export/import transactions is the need for documents traveling between the seller and the buyer to be understood by both parties and yet to still retain their initial functions, including serving as source documents for data entries and audit and control devices. While this can be accomplished with some effort, it does create additional direct and indirect expenses.

Foreign Branch Operations

Because branch activities are closely planned, administered, and controlled by the parent organization, it makes little sense to view the accounts of either in a vacuum. Office-branch accounting has unique aspects that stem from this relationship, such as the existence of reciprocal accounts on the books of both. Foreign currency translation procedures are called for when the branch is in another country and carries its operations in that country's currency.

United States accounting standards require that branch accounts be translated to the parent's currency at the exchange rate prevailing at the end of the reporting period. Gains and losses from translation are deferred through an equity adjustment and do not flow through the net income for the period. Note that the parent and branch accounts are subject to historic accounting, while the branch accounts are translated at current exchange rates. This problem is one of the major controversies surrounding foreign currency translation.

In addition, the branch is subject to rules and regulations of the host country. For example, branches of foreign corporations in Japan are governed by the Commercial Code and the Foreign Exchange and Foreign Trade Control Law. Further, tax regulations require submission of the financial statements of the parent in addition to those of the branch. However, the branch need not publish its financial statements and is not subject to statutory audit requirements.

Foreign Subsidiary Operations

Subsidiary companies enjoy a greater degree of autonomy than branches by virtue of their separate legal existence. Nevertheless, foreign currency translation procedures are required. Financial reports must be consolidated with the parent companies, which continuously monitor the performance of their foreign subsidiaries. Thus, there is a need for accounting information that allows comparisons between subsidiaries' results as well as those of the parent with the consolidated unit. Also, planning and administrative functions of the subsidiary's management cannot be performed effectively unless accounting information has substantially the same basis as the parent's.

At the same time, foreign subsidiaries often rely heavily on local management talent and report to various local government agencies. Therefore, any evaluation of competitive position with local rival companies is difficult unless locally oriented accounting information is also available—so accounting information must also be prepared according to local accounting concepts and practices and in the local currency unit.

General Electric learned an important lesson shortly after taking over a French company in 1988, when it set out to fix the new subsidiary's financial control system. United States computer specialists imposed a GE system that was inappropriate both for French financial reporting requirements and for the subsidiary's existing management practices. The company spent months seeking a workable compromise. In a later acquisition of Tungsram, a Hungarian light-bulb maker, GE worked with local managers to guarantee a smooth transition. It also brought in a manager who was Hungarian-born, U.S.-trained, and a long-time employee of GE to overcome national and corporate cultural conflicts.

International Joint Ventures

Joint ventures are typically characterized by the sharing of technology provided by one participant and production inputs provided by another. Cross-border joint ventures are an efficient way to pool resources, share in risks and rewards, and obtain relatively easy access to a foreign country. In countries such as China, joint ventures are the form of entry preferred by the government. The political and cultural environment dictates both the form of globalization and the accounting system.

International joint ventures are subject to the rules and regulations of the country in which they operate. At the same time, their accounting systems should provide meaningful information to the foreign partners. That can prove to be an enormous task in such countries as the former Soviet Union and Poland. The accounting system in the Soviet Union was designed to provide information, in uniform format, for national economic planners. The joint venture was legally required to keep its books according to the format for Soviet state-owned organizations. Inventory, for example, had to be taken according to Soviet forms and methods. These may not have been suitable for a management information system, creating a situation in which an agreement had to be made with the Soviet authorities so that changes could be made in the accounting system. The joint venture—and its chief bookkeeper—were responsible for observing the procedures and for the reliability of the records. Recall that in the Soviet system, the chief bookkeeper was a high-ranking manager. This led to conflict with foreign managers (expatriates or at the home office) who were accustomed to a more limited and technical role for accountants.

Typically, the joint venture is not a subsidiary of any of the investing parties and is not consolidated on the investors' financial statements. Many American companies invest in joint ventures in countries where opening a subsidiary is either not allowed or not feasible. Frequently in these cases, the local foreign currency is not convertible and a useable exchange rate does not exist. While the dollar value of the initial investment is clearly known, changes in value are difficult to account for on the investors' books. The equity method, which is the method used to account for investment in most U.S. corporate joint ventures, calls for annual adjustment of the value of the investment. Without an acceptable exchange rate, this method may not be possible, and an educated guess may not be enough to convince the company's external auditors. Accounting for the joint venture using the cost method may be more appropriate, but it would lead to reduced economic accuracy of the information presented in the financial statements.

Accounting Information and Global Capital Markets

The number of specific accounting issues that newly globalizing American firms should be aware of is large, and we cannot discuss them all here. We do want to touch on three that are potentially relevant to the management of American firms. The first is the role of American accounting standards in the capital market.

The expanded scale of international investment activities increases the need to convey accounting information about a company domiciled in one country to investors, readers, and users who reside in another. When a company wishes to list its shares on a foreign stock exchange, it has to translate all of its financial statements from the domestic currency to the currency of the exchange's host country. The company may also be subject to accounting adjustments. In the United States the SEC requires that foreign companies wishing to list their shares on American stock exchanges provide disclosure according to U.S. standards, which in many cases go beyond what is required in their home countries. (Some analysts have argued that U.S. firms are penalized when raising capital in international markets because of the additional disclosure requirements.) In recent testimony, the chairman of the SEC rejected a New York Stock Exchange proposal to loosen the listing standards for foreign companies. He claimed that letting foreign firms list in the United States without providing the same disclosure as U.S. companies would seriously disadvantage American firms in their home market.

Raising capital in international markets presents other challenges. Issuers need to provide financial information without distorting the intended message for foreign investors, who need to make decisions about the comparability of prospects based on financial statements prepared according to different languages, currencies, and accounting frameworks. The SEC further defends its position against relaxed reporting standards for foreign firms as providing protection to investors, who might select a foreign company's stock only to discover later that differences in accounting or auditing standards made the firm appear more attractive.

Investors must be able to sort out whether differences in financial measures of risk and return are a function of accounting principles, of the economic or cultural environment, or of real differences in the attributes of the firm. Some analysts argue, for example, that the price to earnings (P/E) ratios of Japanese stocks are relatively high because the economic prospects of Japanese firms (the attributes being measured) are better, either because the cost of funds in Japan is lower or because earnings growth patterns are superior due to Japanese operational efficiencies and product quality. Others argue that the higher P/E ratios are driven by the structure of the Japanese firm (an economic and cultural attribute). Still others would argue that the Japanese accounting system is tax-oriented, and that reported earnings are artificially low (a function of accounting principles), thus leading to a high P/E ratio.

An example of how accounting practices can distort investors' perceptions is that of brand name revaluation, an "aggressive" accounting practice that allows a company to recognize the value of brands it owns as assets. The practice is used by some firms in Britain and Australia, but is not allowed in the United States or by European Community directives. Brand revaluation results in increases to assets and owners' equity, a lower debt to equity ratio, and favorable changes in other accounting-based financial ratios. The revaluing company therefore appears to have a healthier financial position and presumably commands a lower cost of funds in capital markets, although it must also demonstrate a reasonable rate of return on the higher asset base.

Accounting Standards as a Source of Competitive Disadvantage

Many observers claim that the accounting and tax treatment of purchased goodwill in the United States gives foreign firms an unfair advantage when they compete with American companies over potential targets for acquisition. In fact, the "unlevel playing field" argument was suggested as one reason for the explosion of foreign direct investment in the United States in the 1980s. The purchase of Pillsbury by Grand Metropolitan PLC, where an estimated goodwill of four billion dollars was created, is often used as an example of the problem. Although no merger or acquisition can be justified solely on the basis of the accounting or tax treatment of goodwill, it may serve as a deterrent or catalyst in a deal. More important, the perception of inequity is by itself a possible obstacle for the free flow of capital and the global integration of the securities markets.

The accounting and tax treatments for purchased goodwill in selected countries are reported in Table 6.1. In all of these countries, goodwill is defined as the excess of the purchase price over the value of the net assets acquired, where the value is defined as either fair market value (for example, U.S. GAAP) or book value (Japanese GAAP). When goodwill is created by an acquisition, it has to be included in the financial statements of the acquiring firm, reflecting whatever consideration is given in return—cash, other assets, or securities. In the United States, this intangible asset has to be amortized over a period of no more than forty years. Critics claim this mandated practice leads to a lower reported net income for the U.S. firm when compared with a foreign firm (say, British) that is allowed to bypass the income statement and write off

Table 6.1.   Accounting and Tax Treatments for Purchased Goodwill
in Selected Countries

Country[a]	Accounting	Tax
Canada	Goodwill should be amortized over a specified time period.	Tax deductible.
France	Goodwill whould be amortized over useful life.	Tax deductible.
Germany	Goodwill should be carried forward until the subsidiary is disposed of, or value impaired.	Deductible when value is permanently impaired.
Japan	Goodwill should be amortized over an unspecified time period.	Tax deductible.
Netherlands	Goodwill is commonly written off to reserves at year of purchase. Amortization option is available.	Not tax deductible.
United Kingdom	Goodwill may be written against owners' equity.	No tax effect.
United States	Goodwill should be amortized over a specified time period.	Not tax deductible.

[a]The countries include the largest foreign investors in the United States.
Source: Various international accounting and international tax sources.

goodwill against reserves or capitalize it without future amortization. The difference in treatment would lead to less favorable performance measures, such as return on investment (ROI) and other earnings-based ratios, for American firms and their managers.

Another aspect of the "unlevel playing field" is that the amortized amounts are not tax deductible in the United States, but they are in some foreign countries, such as Canada. This situation creates a favorable cash flow for the foreign firm. Thus, an economic advantage exists for those firms whose parent countries subsidize purchased goodwill through tax deductions.

The information from Table 6.1 is presented in an alternative format in Figure 6.1. The countries are assigned to cells according to their accounting and tax attributes. From Figure 6.1 it is clear why U.S. firms seems to be disadvantaged on both the accounting and tax dimensions. The accounting-induced disadvantage results from amortization of goodwill through the income statement, leading to a lower reported net income, while the tax disadvantage is due to the nondeductibility of the amortized amounts.

Of course, if there really are efficient capital markets and sophisti-

Taxation

		Not deductible	Deductible
Accounting	Income statement	United States	Canada France Japan
	Balance sheet	United Kingdom Germany Netherlands	

Figure 6.1 The accounting and tax treatments for purchased goodwill in selected countries.

cated investors, differences in *reported* financial results that do not involve differences in the underlying economic value should not cause a market reaction. Consequently, managers should not consider accounting differences that have no direct cash flow implications when they consider a potential investment. However, when the business press reports that some foreign companies are able to outbid U.S. competitors in acquisition battles because of "favorable" foreign accounting regulations, the widespread belief that this is true may drive down the price of certain U.S. stocks, even though the reduced *reported* income does not reflect a reduced cash flow. The lower reported income may impair a firm's ability to raise capital or to pay dividends. And if the manager's compensation is tied to reported accounting numbers, the manager has an incentive to report higher earnings and avoid transactions that adversely affect the report.

Harmonization of Accounting Standards

Many obstacles on the road to globalization would be removed if there were a standardized format for the presentation of financial statements. Uniformity at the national level has been achieved in France and to a lesser degree in Germany. At the international level, a single uniform accounting system is out of the question for the foreseeable future—and may not even be desirable, given the different environmental factors in each country.

Comparability, however, is not as ambitious a goal as uniformity. Comparability allows for accounting choices but insists that reports coming from different accounting systems have a reasonable basis of comparison. In a letter to the editor of the Wall Street Journal (April 15, 1988), Dennis Beresford, chairman of the Financial Accounting Standards Board (FASB), asked, "Should the objective of accounting standards be to manipulate behavior and effect economic or social change, or to provide relevant and reliable information?" That question must be answered by others. But how does one define "relevant and reliable" information? When comparability is held hostage by differences in national accounting standards, reliability and relevance suffer as well.

There are essentially three models for harmonizing accounting standards, distinguished by the goals of the institutions that drive them: political, professional, and corporate. Examples of the political approach include efforts by the United Nations, the Organization for Economic Cooperation and Development (OECD), and the European Community (EC). The professional approach is backed by the International Accounting Standards Committee (IASC), which sets accounting standards, and the International Federation of Accountants (IFAC), which focuses on audit practices. While the IASC and IFAC are private-sector bodies where membership and compliance are voluntary for each country, the European Commission overseeing the move toward integration in 1992 has regulatory teeth. So far it has issued several directives designed to harmonize financial reporting within the European Community. The evidence indicates that the political/regional approach is working—and the lessons from the EC may be applied to the creation of a Free Trade Zone between Canada, the United States, and Mexico. While it is important to involve the profession in the formulation of standards, the enforcement powers of a political authority give more rapid results.

Regardless of the model, harmonization of accounting standards requires compromises from all parties. Accounting for goodwill once again serves as a prime example. The proposed International Accounting Standard for goodwill would require amortization of the difference between the cost of acquisition and the fair value of the net identifiable assets acquired over five to twenty years. This treatment would cause some American firms to take even bigger hits to net income than the present amounts, which are often based on the maximum forty years of amortization. The proposed standard would penalize many foreign firms as well, since they would have to recognize goodwill amortization on their income statements for the first time. Nevertheless, the standard would yield more comparable information.

Accounting for goodwill is also covered by the fourth and seventh directives from the EC. The fourth directive specifies that goodwill must be written off over five years, with a possible extension to cover its useful life. At the request of the United Kingdom, the seventh directive was devised to allow the immediate writeoff of goodwill against reserves. Ironically, the United Kingdom's Accounting Standards Committee is currently proposing a change in the accounting for goodwill requiring amortization over twenty to forty years, bringing British standards closer to U.S. and proposed international standards. Thus, it appears that there is some movement toward convergence in accounting for goodwill. (Note that the playing field will not be level as long as tax treatments are different.) Similar trends are also present with respect to other accounting standards.

Environmental Factors:	U.S.	Foreign	Divergence
Economic Educational Legal Political Socio-cultural			
System Characteristics: Who sets standards Who are primary users Who enforces standards Level of the profession The audit function			
Accounting Practices: Income measurement Inventory valuation Reserves			
Audit Practices: Balance confirmation Audit risk analysis Audit-related costs			

Figure 6.2 An instrument for comparative analysis.

Integration and Conclusion

In the preceding sections we have discussed the factors that influence national accounting systems and the accounting implications of alternative forms of globalization, describing in detail three central issues. An American firm should be aware of the accounting system in the host country and should avoid shortcuts, such as only becoming acquainted with specific practices that prevail in the new country at a given point in time. Otherwise, the firm will find it difficult to understand and to react to the changes in accounting rules and practices that will surely occur.

To give managers a start on the process, we have included (Figure 6.2), an instrument that can assist the firm as it considers the broad accounting aspects of globalization prospects. The left column contains the attributes of the environment and national system of the parent firm and serves as a benchmark; the middle column, the attributes of the target country; and the third column is the scoring card, where degrees of divergence are noted. The instrument is not designed to provide absolute, quantifiable answers, but simply to serve as a tool to focus management's attention on potential areas of conflict and discord. Managers are encouraged to refine and modify it as they choose, for example to include implementation costs as an element of the evaluation.

REFERENCES

Ewer, S., "A Study of the Effect of Transborder Data Flow Restrictions on U.S. Multinational Corporate Accounting Control Systems," Ph.D. diss., University of Mississippi, 1990.

Farmer, R., and B. Richman, *International Business: An Operational Theory*, Irwin, 1966.

Hofstede, G., "The Cultural Context of Accounting," *Annual Meeting of the American Accounting Association* (B.E. Cushing, ed.), 1986.

Karnes, A., J. Sterner, R. Welker, and F. Wu, "A Bicultural Study of Independent Auditors' Perceptions of Unethical Business Practices," *International Journal of Accounting*, Vol. 24, No. 1, 1989.

Wygal, D.E., D.E. Stout, and J. Volpi, "Reporting Practices in Four Countries," *Management Accounting*, Dec. 1987.

7

United States Trade Laws as Barriers to Globalization

ALAN M. RUGMAN
MICHAEL V. GESTRIN

An axiom of international business states that in order to survive globally, a firm needs to develop a sustainable competitive advantage, usually a proprietary firm-specific advantage (FSA) in technology, management, or marketing skills. The source of the FSA can often be found
within a nation's "diamond" of international competitiveness, to use
Michael Porter's terminology. Porter also explains that FSAs can be reinforced by the use of competition-based entry barriers, which can be
classified according to whether they are cost reducing or differentiation
enhancing. These strategies are ultimately efficiency based and capable
of increasing national economic welfare.

But firms can also pursue strategies that involve the use of national
policies and laws to erect shelter-based (discriminatory) entry barriers
against foreign, rival companies. These shelter-seeking strategies do not
generate sustainable competitive advantages, are inefficient, and reduce
the national economic welfare. We will use the United States as an
example to explain this thesis.

The U.S. Congress is designed to reflect regional and special interests. It is subject to intensive lobbying by both domestic- and foreign-
interest groups. We have been involved in research (along with Alain
Verbeke and Andrew Anderson) establishing that domestic groups seek-

ing shelter have captured the administration of U.S. trade-remedy laws (countervailing duty and anti-dumping actions), and that the test of "material injury" due to allegedly subsidized or dumped imports is therefore determined more by political considerations than by scientific economics. United States firms have a high success rate in their efforts to achieve administered protection and have effectively erected a shelter-based, non-tariff barrier to entry against foreign firms in the same industry. The importance of this is illustrated by the fact that U.S. firms file more than 90 percent of all the world's countervail actions.

Shelter strategies can be divided between those on the "technical track" and those on the "high track." The high track directly involves the government and official diplomatic channels between countries. Examples of high track protectionism include Voluntary Export Restraints (VERs) such as those in imports of autos, steel, and semiconductors. Another example, although not specific to the United States, is the institutionalized protectionism for textile and clothing products inherent in the Multi-Fibres Arrangement.

Technical track strategies use available bureaucratic and legal mechanisms to raise entry barriers for foreign competitors. These mechanisms include countervailing duties (CVDs), anti-dumping duties (ADs), and safeguard actions.

The development of FSAs in technology, management, or marketing skills bears costs that are discounted by a firm against future anticipated returns from the improvements. But the same logic does not apply to shelter-based entry barriers. Shelter-based entry barriers are not needed by a firm that uses efficiency-based cost-reducing or differentiation-enhancing advantages. In fact, shelter strategies not only fail to develop sustainable FSAs, they can serve to undermine them.

The competitiveness of a firm or industry is determined by its strategic use of cost-reducing and differentiation-enhancing FSAs. If an industry has little potential in this area, shelter strategies will serve to secure a share of the protected domestic market that it would otherwise lose. However, for an industry that does enjoy cost-reducing or differentiation-enhancing potential, shelter-based entry barriers are unnecessary and limit the industry to the protected domestic market, excluding it from the share of the global market that a development of competitive advantages would otherwise permit.

In other words, shelter-based entry barriers are not to be treated like any other input. They are not subject to the type of cost-benefit analysis that guides firms in their allocations between labor and capital, for example. Rather, they are a second-best strategy, the feasibility of which is dependent upon a firm's capacity to establish those barriers. Figure 7.1 illustrates the relationship between these two types of corporate strategy.

Indeed, shelter-based strategies provide only a temporary barrier to entry. Sheltered U.S. firms attempt to turn their backs on globalization.

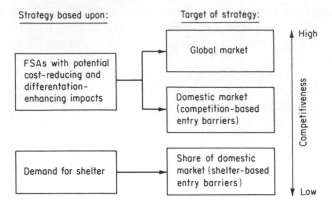

Figure 7.1 The relationship between types of corporate strategy.

They use the political system to postpone the economic adjustments required to generate sustainable FSAs. Nevertheless, there is a strong protectionist culture in the United States that attempts to rationalize shelter-based strategies. In contrast, in small, open, trading economies such as that of Canada, this protectionist mindset is being abandoned, leaving firms in these nations better placed to take advantage of the opportunities for globalization. Thus Canada was more concerned with achieving redress against the perceived abuse of U.S. trade law actions than was the U.S. during the negotiations for the Canada–U.S. Free Trade Agreement.

Shelter-based strategies unfortunately suffer from the tragedy of the commons. That is, the manager who chooses not to graze upon protectionist pastures offered by government and bureaucracy will lose out in the short run to competitors who do take advantage of such opportunities. But when an industry pursues this strategy, globalization is impeded and competitiveness diminished.

Contrary to the prescriptions of the new literature on strategic trade policy, we have concluded that government must limit, not increase, its involvement in trade. Strategic targeting is simply not feasible within the context of a highly decentralized system such as that in the United States. Only in more centralized economic systems, such as that of Japan, can the state join with business in FSA-creating policies.

The Political Economy of Protection

Two broad themes dominate the literature on protectionism. The first concerns the relationship between industry characteristics and the amount of protection provided by government. The second looks into the relationship between industry characteristics and the type of protection, technical or high track.

The factors that have the greatest impact upon the amount of protection supplied to an industry include size, firm concentration, geographic location, and labor intensity of production. For example, a large industry will be able to mobilize greater resources for its directly unproductive activities. Conversely, if the industry is fragmented, higher organizational costs and the free-rider problem will hamper its lobbying efforts.

Less is known about the effect of industry characteristics upon the type of protection. Generally, however, most industries have had to be satisfied with the technical track (AD and CVD), while only a few particularly powerful industries have been able to establish high-track protectionist arrangements. In other words, up to a certain critical mass of lobbying power, all industries can affect the levels of protection they receive within the confines of the technical track, but only the largest can push for a broader set of protectionist instruments.

As mentioned earlier, industries that have won high-track protection include autos, steel, electronics, and textiles and clothing. In these industries, the products have characteristics that make the technical track less effective. The textile and clothing industry is a case in point. Anti-dumping and countervailing duties were considered to provide insufficient protection for three main reasons.

The first was that textiles and clothing are highly undifferentiated, which allows for easy trans-shipment (that is, exporting products from one country to another via a third). By this ploy an exporter avoids AD measures, which target particular industries in particular countries, and CVDs, which target products from particular countries.

The second reason for the ineffectiveness of the technical track is the low start-up cost and small recoupment period that characterize textile and clothing production. The industry is therefore highly mobile and difficult to target with relatively precise trade instruments such as ADs and CVDs.

A third characteristic of textile and apparel production that complicates protectionist policies is mutability. An example would be the conversion of a jacket, on which a duty is imposed, into a vest and sleeves, on which there are no duties, with a view to having the jacket reassembled in the importing country.

The iron and steel industry is an example of a situation in which the technical track has been effective. There are high costs associated with the transportation of the industry's two main inputs, iron ore and coal, both of which are characterized by extremely high weight-to-value ratios. Furthermore, the physical capital for this industry is expensive and heavy, requiring extremely high start-up costs and long recoupment periods. Thus, this industry has been easily targeted by ADs and CVDs, later reinforced by the VER quotas.

To further explain the difference, there were 417 AD cases and 322 CVD cases brought by U.S. firms between 1980 and 1988. Whether looked at in terms of absolute number of cases brought, or cases weighted by value of imports, the iron and steel industry is by far the most frequent user. This industry, in fact, has a history of using both the technical and the high tracks to develop shelter-based strategies. In contrast, the apparel and clothing industry used neither AD nor CVD from 1980 to 1988, but pursued only high-track shelter strategies.

Protection can be thought of as a commodity that is produced by the government and demanded by industry. The price of protection for industry consists of the various costs associated with acquiring it: legal fees, the costs of maintaining a strong lobby, and so on. The cost to the government of producing protection, on the other hand, consists of the potential loss of votes due to higher consumer prices, the potential loss of international authority where protectionist policies damage legitimacy, the financial and bureaucratic costs of operating a system in which the treatment of goods in trade is highly differentiated, and so on. The cost to the government of not producing protection is embodied in the loss of political support that accompanies high levels of unemployment.

In a study of the textiles, steel, and automobile industries in the United States, William Cline found that the two factors most likely to explain protection were the size of a given industry's labor force and the level (not the rate) of import penetration. A more general study by Wendy Takacs identified the factors contributing the most to protectionist pressure as the merchandise trade balance, import penetration, a "demonstration" effect (defined as the success rate for petitions in the previous year), and legislative dummies (which serve to identify the effects of key trade acts). She further identified the factors that contributed the most to actual protection, not just pressure for protection, as the size of the trade deficit and the degree of import penetration.

The very threat of protection shapes trading patterns. The possibility that a firm or industry might file a trade complaint acts as an impediment to trade because foreign producers must incorporate this additional risk into their cost functions. The costs increase both with the probability that the case would be launched as well as with the actual costs of the case. Because of this, foreign producers will raise prices just to avoid charges of dumping.

Recent Evolution of the Technical Track

In 1985, the Trade Agreements Program of the Reagan Administration outlined a new three-track trade strategy, partly to supplement the post-WWII cornerstone of U.S. trade policy, the multilateral General Agreement on Tariffs and Trade (GATT) system. While multilateralism through the GATT would continue to play a role, it would be a considerably diminished one. The two other tracks were a policy of establishing bilateral free trade agreements and a much-expanded role for the use of Section 301 of the 1974 Trade Act against unfair trade practices (namely dumping). Therefore, as Sylvia Ostry put it, "Despite the continuing support for the Uruguay Round, neither the United States government nor the business community accepts any longer the preservation and strengthening of liberal multilateral trade as a single, overriding objective."

The primary significance of these developments to American firms was that the traditional distinction in U.S. trade policy between high- and technical-track trade policy was becoming increasingly blurred. In the Annual Report of the President of the United States on the Trade Agreements Program for 1984–1985, a much more active role for the government in the administration of the technical track was described.

Underlying this heightened government intervention at the technical-track level was the growing sense in Washington of the inadequacy of the GATT's definitions of unfairness, combined with the perception that it was foreign governments, not necessarily foreign companies, that were the main practitioners of unfair trade practices. Ultimately the effect of these developments was to send a strong message to American industry that first, the technical track would be much more active with the participation of the United States Trade Representative's Office (USTR) as "the negotiating 'combat' agency for trade issues," as Earl Grinols described it, and second, that complaints launched by industry on this track would probably receive a more sympathetic hearing than had been the case in the past.

Industry support for the effectiveness of the technical track was further bolstered with the Omnibus Trade and Competitiveness Act of 1988 (OTCA), which further increased the likelihood that dumping or countervail investigations would end in findings of unfair trade practices. In fact, the OTCA announced that cases would now be launched against "priority" countries and practices. This clause has been interpreted in practice as one aimed mainly at Japan's bilateral trade balance with the United States, leading to the Structural Impediments Initiatives of 1990. The key criterion toward determining "priority" has been bilateral balance of payments on the current account with trading partners.

Another important aspect of the OTCA for firms pursuing discriminatory shelter was that it gave the Department of Commerce unprecedented discretionary powers to take retaliatory action against exporters suspected of practicing "circumvention." This practice is described by Ostry as consisting of avoiding AD and CVDs by producing in third countries, making minor changes to products, and relocating the assembly of parts to either third countries or the importer itself.

In summary, the U.S. technical track has changed considerably since

1985. Enforcement of technical-track rules has tightened, and their use and application has been facilitated. The line between technical track and high track has blurred. Whereas the technical track traditionally served to deflect protectionist pressures away from politicians, the government's decision to break this barrier by becoming a player in the process meant that the firms would now be able to increase shelter by drawing the government directly into their trading disputes.

The new strategy has already had an effect. From 1985 to 1988, the U.S. government threatened to self-initiate cases twenty-six times against ten of its trading partners. In eighteen of these instances, the mere threat was sufficient to extract concessions, and the cases themselves were never launched. The period from 1985 to 1988 therefore witnessed a rapid evolution of the technical track into a much more viable source of protection for U.S. industry. These developments will not position U.S. firms to do well in a world of global competition. For example, although the U.S. steel industry has developed some efficient "minimills," it is still reliant on VERs and is basically dependent on subsidies.

Conclusions

We have argued that corporate economic performance is the outcome of a combination of two types of corporate strategy. On the one hand, corporations can seek to develop firm-specific advantages that are either cost reducing or differentiation enhancing. If successful, this strategy leads to competition-based entry barriers. On the other hand, corporations can seek to establish shelter-based entry barriers. Most industries pursue some combination of these strategies.

The pursuit of shelter-based entry barriers slows the process of globalization. One reason for this is that the pursuit of directly unproductive activities diverts considerable resources from activities that aim at cost reduction and differentiation enhancement. For example, one million dollars spent on an AD case is one million dollars not spent on research and development. Another important reason is that by limiting imports, competition, which is the cornerstone of the globalization process, is also limited.

The U.S. economy suffers from a structural impediment to globalization arising from a political system that is highly decentralized and thus sensitive to pressures from various lobbying groups. Given that it is perfectly rational from the individual firm's perspective to pursue a shelter-based strategy as part of its overall corporate strategy (especially if it cannot produce competition-based entry barriers), then the onus for limiting the use of these strategies is not upon the firm, but upon the government.

The U.S. government's increasing willingness to become directly involved in trade disputes using the technical track has been particularly disturbing because that track traditionally served the purpose of protecting the politically sensitive executive branch in U.S. politics from all but the most powerful lobbies—those that were able to jump from the technical track to the high track. Now the executive branch, including the President, will be exposed to protectionist pressures from a much wider cross-section of U.S. corporate society. Furthermore, some industries have shown signs of successfully using the technical track to pressure government to move more forcefully on their behalf on the high track. The iron and steel sector is a case in point: By overloading the technical track, it has pushed government to act on the high track.

Hence, the increasingly political nature of the technical track threatens the globalization of the U.S. economy in two ways. First, it gives traditional high-track actors (autos, semiconductors, iron and steel, and so on) one more lever with which to exercise a shelter-based strategy. Second, it gives smaller players an opportunity to pursue shelter through the technical track when they might not have done so before because the relevant political actors could not have been brought on side. Crucial to limiting the negative effects of both the technical and high tracks on continued globalization will be more research on the relationship of these instruments to the decline of U.S. corporate competitiveness.

REFERENCES

Cline, W.R., "U.S. Trade and Industrial Policy: The Experience of Textiles, Steel, and Automobiles," *Strategic Trade Policy and the New International Economics* (P.R. Krugman, ed.), MIT Press, 1986.

Grinols, E.L., "Procedural Protectionism: The American Trade Bill and the New Interventionist Mode," *Weltwirtschaftliches Archiv*, Vol. 125, No. 3, 1989.

Ostry, S., *Government and Corporations in a Shrinking World: Trade and Innovation Policies in the United States, Europe and Japan,* Council on Foreign Relations, 1989.

Porter, M., *Competitive Advantage of Nations,* Free Press, 1990.

Takacs, W.E., "Pressures for Protectionism: An Empirical Analysis," *Economic Enquiry*, Vol. 19, 1981.

8

Negotiating the Initial Phases of Cross-Cultural Alliances

KATHLEEN K. REARDON
ROBERT SPEKMAN

To paraphrase John Donne, no corporation is an island. Just as people are linked by common concerns over such matters as pollution and world hunger, and countries form alliances for military protection and economic well-being, businesses today also find their fortunes inextricably bound with one another—with ties frequently crossing national borders.

Richard Drobnick has identified six world trends that gathered strength in the late 1980s and will shape the economic environment of the 1990s:

1. the evolution of U.S.–Soviet relations from conflict to cooperation;
2. the collapse of communism in the Soviet Union and Eastern Europe;
3. the reversal of America's "locomotive" role in the world economy;
4. the ascendancy of Japan as the world's banker;
5. the economic integration of Europe;
6. the economic integration of North America.

To adapt to these changes, organizations will have to consider partnerships outside their own geographical areas. Going it alone is difficult under any circumstances, because it means a corporation must have the ability to do all things well. As Kenichi Ohmae argues, "With enough time, money and luck you can expand brands and build up distribution yourself—you can do everything yourself. But all three are in short supply."

Intercompany alliances—in many cases cross-cultural alliances—provide an answer. These alliances are not to be confused with the hostile takeovers that raged like brushfires across the corporate landscape of the 1980s. The employees who made the businesses worth acquiring in the first place frequently either left or became too demoralized to function as inspired, devoted members of a team with a shared vision. The replacements for those who left, some willingly but some not, were seldom familiar with the company culture or the culture of the surrounding area.

Alliances, to work, must be what the term "allies" suggests: a collaboration between two parties for the betterment of both. But this sense of reciprocity has all too often been lost. Many organizations view their cross-cultural alliances as quick and inexpensive ways to get a foothold in the global marketplace. Unfortunately, this cheap, self-serving philosophy is destroying the majority of strategic alliances.

Most alliances fail because the relationship is poorly planned from the outset. Companies enamored by the prospect of a relationship of convenience with few strings trip over the one unyielding fact about all relationships: There is no such thing as a long-term relationship without commitment. Without planning, negotiation of differences, establishment of trust and respect, and a sense of mutual benefit, a relationship has little promise after the infatuation wears off.

Many American managers have an unfortunate tendency to see the interpersonal communication aspects of business as "soft," as something that will work out just fine if the numbers are right. It does not happen. Tandy broke off a relationship with the U.K. firm Apricot Computors when it became clear that the companies had not communicated how their marketing strategies would be combined. They had no relationship history to draw on, and conflict surfaced shortly after the venture was formed.

The key to any effective alliance is skillful management of the relationship from the initial handshake forward. In cross-cultural alliances the challenge is greater, since each party sees the negotiation through a different lens.

The French are proud of their reasoned discussions. They dislike being rushed into decisions, preferring to examine all options carefully. Negotiations are likely to be in French, especially if held on·their soil. They expect punctuality, and they tend to be formal.

In Japan, business often goes to the party that inspires the most respect. But recognizing who deserves the respect—and the business—

takes more time than Americans like to give. Moreover, the Japanese consult everyone involved before making a decision. If a delivery date is specified, they are likely to check with the managers who will be responsible for meeting it before agreeing. They ask detailed questions about financial, marketing, manufacturing, and structural issues, all relevant to them, if not necessarily to an outsider. The Japanese also spend time simply getting to know the potential partner.

American negotiators operate as if today is the last day of their lives. They argue with conviction and interpret delays or hesitations as signs of stalling or ineptitude. Most speak only English. Ford, for example, has a complex alliance with Mazda, but no employee involved speaks fluent Japanese. Many U.S. managers are hesitant about the whole idea of alliances—alliances are viewed as frequently ineffective and potentially dangerous. Americans are capable of developing long-term relationships characterized by respect and mutual consideration, but an outsider might not realize it from their words and behaviors, which are perceived as tough and insensitive. Vince Lombardi spoke for the American psyche when he said that winning isn't everything, it's the only thing. But once assured they will not lose, American negotiators can be redirected toward mutual gains.

Bridging such differences cannot be accomplished without effort. There must be a strong desire to make things work and the ability to see the differences as stemming from other cultural patterns, not as sure signs of incompatibility or threats to control.

Developing Rapport

"Know how the other person thinks" is the fundamental tenet of negotiation. But American managers who believe that "time is money" may be reluctant to make the investment necessary to understand alliance partners. So alliances such as those between GEC and Germany's Siemens (forged to take over Plessey, a British electronics defense firm) or AT&T and Olivetti (more about this one later) fail, in large part, because the people involved differ in style and temperament. Roland Smith, of British Aerospace, was quoted in *Fortune,* "There's a certain amount of tension and you have to accept that there will be differences. You have to cultivate alliances and take the time, not just to give instructions but to create the right environment."

Creating the right environment in Sweden, however, is not the same as doing so in Italy. For example, the Swedes tend to be formal, dislike haggling over price, expect thorough, professional, flawless proposals, and are attracted to quality. Italians tend to be hospitable and volatile. They make their points emotionally, with much gesticulation. They enjoy haggling over prices and are impressed by style.

Individual Swedes or Italians will, of course, violate the stereotypes.

But they demonstrate how people from different cultures come to negotiating sessions with different expectations and styles of conducting business. A foreign negotiator who is blind to these differences will create a negative impression that, once formed, is an almost impassable barrier to rapport.

Sequent Computer Systems Inc. has imbued its Beaverton, Oregon, headquarters with an international flavor to encourage cross-cultural rapport. President Scott Gibson named office buildings after foreign rivers and conference rooms after overseas cities. Managers attend European business schools. The payoff has been a 64 percent jump in international sales, to $23.3 million in the first quarter of 1991.

The process of building rapport is based on subtle cues, in which actions speak louder than words. An American businessman who gave a clock as a wedding present to the daughter of his Chinese counterpart—not realizing that in China clocks are associated with death—not only failed to establish rapport, but caused the termination of the business relationship. An Arab businessman who insists on giving his Japanese counterpart gifts of greater value than those he receives harms the alliance before it begins.

There are no trivial actions when people are forming impressions. Hewlett Packard spent years slowly and deliberately building its Japanese relationships. It recognized early on that it would need to take time to nurture the relationships, and that patience was essential to building trust and mutual confidence. HP genuinely wanted to serve its Japanese customers. Control was not an issue. HP now has a significant presence in the Japanese market.

Some questions to ask when developing rapport with an alliance partner are:

- Have we developed a climate of trust?
- Are we satisfied with our own and their level of commitment?
- How similar are our cultures?
- Is cultural adaptation possible and desirable?
- Do we have a strategy for merging different management styles?
- Have we given adequate attention to credibility and rapport at every interface?

Expectations

Whether an alliance is within or across cultures, partners must be aware of and understand each other's expectations. Checkpoints must be established so that partners have some identifiable means of determining whether those expectations are being met.

Like Hewlett Packard, Coca Cola knew that penetrating the Japanese market would take time. The channels of distribution were more complex than those in the United States and were reluctant to open to foreign companies. So Coca Cola courted local distributors and kept its vision focused not on short-term profits but on long-term expectations. The reward for its patience and adaptability has been a 70 percent market share.

The story of the alliance between AT&T and Olivetti, on the other hand, is a cautionary one. On December 21, 1983, AT&T announced it was purchasing 25 percent of Olivetti (100 million shares) for $260 million. The agreement specified that after four years of 25 percent ownership, AT&T would have an option for the next five years to increase its percentage to 40 percent. It looked like a good deal for both sides. Importantly, AT&T could establish a presence in Europe. Beyond that, AT&T believed that the explosion in information technology would culminate in the merging of telecommunications with office computer and information systems. The company had the communications know-how but lacked the desktop products. Olivetti had the products. Olivetti also stood to gain marketing and manufacturing rights for AT&T telecommunications equipment sold in Europe and a boost to the low sales of its U.S. unit. The firm had twenty other minority buy-ins with U.S. companies as of late 1982 and was hoping to challenge IBM's dominance in the office automation market.

The bright future of the alliance was quickly tarnished by signs of poor communication. While onlookers speculated about the development of a joint Olivetti/AT&T personal computer, the basic arrangement faltered. An Olivetti announcement that AT&T had agreed to buy $250 million of products was countered by AT&T's statement in the Wall Street Journal that "AT&T may sell Olivetti products in the U.S. in the future but . . . no decision on specific products has yet been made."

Communication problems were apparent again in April 1988 in conflicting accounts of an AT&T attempt to gain a larger share of Olivetti. The story in Italy was that Olivetti had successfully fended off a coup. United States sources argued that cash-poor Olivetti had initiated the AT&T move. Clearly, no matter which story was correct, the alliance was on a rocky road.

Throughout its existence, the AT&T/Olivetti alliance suffered from rumors and breakdowns in communication—most stemming from AT&T's limited experience in managing international relationships. While IBM generated 40 percent of its $33 billion 1985 sales outside the United States, AT&T had only 1 percent of its $26 billion 1985 sales coming from outside. AT&T computers and office switchboards were selling slowly in Europe, and its goal of 20 percent European annual sales growth was out of reach.

Despite attempts to appear united, Olivetti's disappointment with AT&T's marketing of its products in the United States and AT&T's displeasure with Olivetti's European sales of its 3B2 computers and System

75 telephone switchboard lines were evident. And when Olivetti developed a line of minicomputers that competed directly with the AT&T machines it was supposed to sell, break-up became inevitable.

Before entering into an alliance, certain questions regarding expectations should be addressed:

- Do we know the key resource gaps facing the venture?
- Have objectives been realistically linked to resources?
- Have major strategic issues and challenges been identified?
- Have key business risks been uncovered?
- Have we performed an analysis of the strengths and weaknesses of each partner?
- Do they understand our expectations and do we understand theirs?
- Have we protected ourselves, as much as possible, from breakdowns in communication that will mask shifts in expectations?

Communication

The AT&T/Olivetti alliance illustrates how important communication is in the early stages of alliance formation. Establishing a shared identity requires trust and mutual respect, neither of which is obtainable unless both parties represent their intentions clearly. Cross-cultural alliances require communication strategies that deal specifically with both present and potential mismatches between partner expectations.

When Ford and IVECO started a joint venture to produce trucks in Britain, expectations and responsibilities were made clear from the outset. Key positions were given to people who could effectively manage the interface. The close, trusting relationships between upper management at Ford and IVECO set the pattern for subordinates. Plans were developed to facilitate information flows at critical junctures. In contrast, the Uniroyal and Goodrich joint venture failed because the two companies neglected to mesh operations and accounting systems.

Sensitivity to the subtleties of intercompany relationships is fundamental to success. A firm that finds memos offensive, for example, will not respond well to a partner who considers them the most efficient and effective means of conveying information. Partners who are always checking their backs to see if each is stealing the other's ideas will soon be operating alone. And if the people selected to manage the alliance are not multicultural in outlook, preferably fluent in each other's languages, no amount of communication planning will facilitate a successful alliance.

Olivetti and AT&T might have fared better had they taken more time to learn about each other, had they communicated more frequently, and had they operated like team members. Communications crises are prob-

ably inevitable in cross-cultural alliances, but proper planning can reduce the discomfort and head off the destruction.

Going into the alliance, certain questions must be asked:

• How frequently should we communicate?
• Who will communicate with whom?
• What forms of communication are appropriate (telephone, memos, meetings, and so on)?
• What types of information will be shared?
• What types of information are proprietary?
• How will we deal with communication problems?
• What aspects of our respective company cultures might hinder communication?

Power

Alliances do not flourish in a competitive environment. They do not
prosper without cooperative decision making, and they suffer without
mutual commitment and participation. Alliance formation requires
abandoning an "I call the shots" management style for a focus on consensus, a dependence on persuasion rather than manipulation or coer-
cion.

Negotiators who are power-oriented show deference to those in
power, are prone to "correct" thinking, tend to be cynical and sus-
picious, and act in a less cooperative manner than those without such
traits, according to Rubin and Brown. In fact, these negotiators are
inclined to see attempts at consensus as indications of weakness. But
such people often represent U.S. businesses because they flatter the
bosses who select negotiators and because they appear tough-minded.
Their selection hinders negotiations across cultural boundaries before
they begin. Their inflexibility impedes discussions of alternatives, and
their tendency to undervalue people they do not perceive as having
status and power leads to behaviors that insult their negotiation counterparts. Their unwillingness to participate in a process of finding the
best course of action rather than a process of adhering to "correct"
choices further damages their mission.

Most U.S. companies have hierarchical structures. Someone is the
boss. The emphasis is on control rather than planning, and on decisive-
ness rather than patient deliberations. Participative management is
touted in U.S. journals and taught in business schools, but only the
illusion of participative management exists in most U.S. organizations. It
is not easy for a society that values individualistic, shoot-from-the-hip
leaders to shift to a style that requires what Warren Bennis describes as
the ability to empower others. Choosing empowerment means that
leaders must have sufficient self-confidence to relinquish the trappings

of control. They must also have what Max DePree sees as a willingness to be vulnerable.

Vulnerability is actually nothing new for U.S. companies entering into cross-cultural alliances. But this is not the voluntary kind of vulnerability to which DePree refers. Instead, U.S. companies are vulnerable because their limited knowledge of alliance partners' languages and cultures puts them at a disadvantage. They may possess the appearance of power by maintaining majority control of the venture on paper, but in reality many lose power through ignorance.

Corning has entered into a number of alliances based on equal shares and mutual interdependence. Much of the success of the Corning-Samsung TV-bulb venture (third largest in the world) is because of the fifty-fifty arrangement. Both partners have an equal commitment and must work hard to solve the joint problems. By contrast, asymmetry breeds instability. William Ouchi calls equity the cornerstone in building long-term relationships. Where equity does not exist, opportunistic behaviors take hold. One partner's gains are the other's losses.

To avoid the undesirable effects of asymmetry, farsighted companies recognize that power has less to do with the percentage of ownership in a joint venture than it does with mutual dependency. An equation is often used to describe power in terms of dependency:

$$\text{Power (A over B)} = \text{Dependence (B on A)}$$

To the extent that alliance partners depend on each other for some commodity or service, for example, they are likely to share power. If one partner is completely dependent on the other, power is unequally distributed. While the latter scenario might work, the former is the more stable recipe for an alliance. Therefore it behooves each partner to identify the assets they have that might be attractive to another and to pursue alliances to tap into knowledge and resources that lie outside the boundary of the firm, to share the risks for activities beyond the scope or capability of a single firm, and to attract complementary skills.

For example, Singapore Shipyard has financial resources and business connections, but it lacks managers. A potential alliance partner who brings management expertise and the promise of training to the table may prove influential. This approach was taken by AT&T when it arranged for a group of Chinese decision-makers to spend several months at major U.S. business schools at AT&T's expense. The Chinese hunger for education is insatiable. Recognizing this, AT&T paved the way for future alliances with its gift.

Information is often overlooked as a source of power. Rosabeth Moss Kanter argues that two types of information are required for effective partnership participation: "technical knowledge, which permits contributions to decision-making, and 'relationship' knowledge— understanding of the partner, knowledge of partnership activities, political intelligence—that provides the background for successful negotiations." Kanter attributes Japanese success at assimilating their U.S. partners' skills to their knowledge of English and of U.S. culture. They effectively bridge the information gap that places U.S. companies at a disadvantage. They understand their partners' needs and demonstrate their ability to meet those needs. By knowing more about their partners than is known about them, they have a form of power in their alliances not easily identifiable by managers who define power in terms of ownership or toughness of style. In the absence of accurate and adequate information about a partner, a company can never have confidence that everyone is playing on a level field. It is impossible to empower others or open oneself to vulnerability without information. Knowing one's partners well is power.

The following guidelines will help in distributing power to the advantage of alliance partners:

- Identify clearly what each partner brings to the table.
- Be sure that the negotiators selected are multicultural in orientation, knowledgeable of the partner's interests and needs, flexible with regard to exploring alternatives, and trained in participative management.
- Nurture a culture of cooperation and mutual benefit.
- Where equity in ownership is not possible or desirable, work to assure that equity in concern for partner benefits exists.
- Where possible, delegate authority and empower others. Let local managers take responsibility for reaching alliance goals.

Persuasion

Once expectations are matched, communication structures are in place, and the partner is becoming a known quantity, the real work of cross-cultural alliances begins. That work involves persuasion.

In spite of what dictionaries may say, persuasion is not something one does *to* another. Persuasion is done *with* others, as a result of cooperative effort, a give-and-take process that requires a willingness to learn what the other has to give and hopes to take. Graham and Sano propose that the U.S. business negotiator's tendency to "get to the point" is responsible for many failures: "We don't teach our students how to ask questions, how to listen, or how to use questioning as a powerful persuasive strategy. In fact, few of us realize that in most places in the world, the one who asks questions controls the process of negotiation and thereby accomplishes more in bargaining situations."

The three essential persuasion steps in the negotiation of cross-cultural alliances are motivation, participation, and reward. To start with, the parties involved must be motivated to reach what persuasion researchers call "private acceptance." That means it is not enough for partners simply to comply with agreed-upon guidelines for the alliance; they must believe in them and actively promote adherence to them. McDonald's seeks fifty-fifty relationships in foreign countries not just to preserve a balance of power, but because management believes that such equality motivates its partners to be more aggressive and innovative in promoting the joint venture.

Effective negotiators operate like detectives searching for clues to the values and interests of their counterparts. They avoid assumptions about their partners' concerns. They look for what *does* matter rather than what *should* matter. The American negotiator who thinks a Saudi counterpart should be more concerned with time efficiency and less with hospitality and rapport is in for a big surprise. A contract full of U.S. legalese is likely to cause offense to Japanese negotiators, implying that their motives are suspect even before the venture starts.

Since the best form of persuasion is self-persuasion, it is important to encourage participation in alliance goals. People become comfortable with new behaviors after they have observed themselves doing new things and succeeding at them. They are then motivated to continue.

American Airlines knew the importance of participation when management involved employees in changing their culture to be more customer-oriented. The carrier implemented an "internal marketing strategy" that involved persuading employees that they are part of the chain to the customer and that their actions must be guided by customer needs and interests. Nearly ten years before, American Airlines had launched a "quality of work life" program to encourage employee participation and a sense of ownership. And an employee suggestion program initiated three years ago has not only encouraged employees to solve problems, but has generated savings for the company of $113 million.

The key to successful participation is training—both of workers and of managers. Despite an increased interest in participative management in Asian countries, implementation of change is hindered by a lack of university-educated workers (6 percent in Singapore, 16 percent in Japan, compared with 23 percent in the United States). Managers must be trained to listen—one of the greatest managerial challenges—and to empower their employees to make decisions. A frequent employee complaint is that managers do not listen to them. This suggests that establishing true participative management in a company is likely to be difficult. In cross-cultural alliances, the challenge is even greater, but well worth the effort.

Reward is the third step in the persuasion process. Since people do not change behaviors easily, and do not stick with the change easily, they need tangible signs of progress. For some, praise is enough. Others need more. Alliance partners should identify methods for rewarding each other and their employees. For example, GE and SNECMA adjusted their revenue-sharing formula to account for unexpected changes in exchange rates and inflation. GE admits the action was not altogether altruistic: self-serving behavior would eventually hurt the company by damaging the relationship. Generally, rewards should be based on a long-term view, not on short-term profits. Reward structures should emphasize joint problem-solving, communication, and relationship-building activities.

Some persuasion guidelines for cross-cultural alliances are:

- Identify similarities and differences between partners with regard to what motivates each to want a successful alliance.
- Find ways to involve all employees in the success of the alliance.
- Train managers from both companies to encourage employee participation in decision making.
- Select a participative management program that meets the needs and possibilities of partner companies.
- Establish a reasonable time frame for implementation of participative management.
- Develop an internal marketing strategy for disseminating policy information so that employees are kept informed.
- Develop reward systems that focus on employee contributions to the success of the alliance.

Negotiation Strategy

Before sitting down to work out the details of an alliance, negotiators should give some thought to how the partner should be approached, what can be given away, and what must remain nonnegotiable. Time is needed to learn the styles of the key people involved in the development of the alliance. Do their styles mesh with ours? Are they willing to discuss concessions? Is conflict likely? How will we handle it?

As Fisher and Ury recommend, the initial focus should be on reconciling interests rather than on taking positions or making demands. Objectives should be introduced and the merits of each discussed. In cross-cultural negotiations in particular, it is important to ask for help in understanding the reasons for objectives that seem at odds with one's own.

While the purpose of early discussions is information gathering, it is sometimes appropriate to introduce a plan, explaining that the offer is tentative, and seeking a response from the partner. This leaves the door open to change without putting anyone in a face-losing position. When concessions must be made, effective negotiators will make those that can be made comfortably, but offer resistance on others without closing off the discussion. They do not dismiss apparently unreasonable offers or proposals out-of-hand. They treat all suggestions as if they have merit or are backed by some logic that is clear to the other party.

Strong-arm tactics are counterproductive, since the way to establish a long-term relationship is through attending to both partners' interests. Here are some additional strategies for the early phase of alliance negotiation:

- If your partner must make an uncomfortable concession, find a way to compensate.
- Express disagreements in terms of difficulties (time contraints, limited resources, established policies) rather than as refusals.
- Return to agreed-upon objectives as reasons for your proposals or your inability to accept theirs.
- Seek your partner's perspective frequently, making sure that your reasons are understood.
- Offer alternatives that meet the other's concerns.
- Avoid value judgments.
- Take time to reflect on proposals and positions.
- Observe tone and style changes.
- Back up proposals with evidence of their feasibility.

Conclusion

Cross-cultural alliances often fail because of poor communication in the early phases of negotiation. Sometimes one partner enters the alliance intending to gain information and leave, but most are entered into with the hope of establishing a long-term, prosperous relationship. This requires attention, patience, and not just tolerance for differences in culture, but rather an appreciation of those differences.

Such appreciation does not happen overnight. Some skepticism regarding the likelihood of success of even the most promising potential alliance is in order, because the intermingling of cultures is a delicate matter. Getting off to a strong start helps, because a solid foundation can weather the inevitable doubts, misunderstandings, and conflicts. Ohmae warns that as time goes on, most partners begin to find fault with each other. They convince themselves they could do better alone, forgetting or minimizing the benefits. If these relationships also suffer from poor initial planning, mismatched expectations, poor communication, inequitable power distribution, and inadequate negotiation of objectives, the decline is likely to be rapid. A successful alliance requires skillful management from the beginning and a willingness to break free from the ethnocentrism that limits potential as it limits perspective.

REFERENCES

Bennis, W., *Why Leaders Can't Lead*, Jossey-Bass, 1989.

DePree, M., *Leadership Is an Art*, Doubleday, 1989.

Drobnick, R., "America and the Pacific Rim—1991 and Beyond," paper presented at the Asia/Pacific Business Outlook Conference, Los Angeles, 1991.

Fisher, R., and W. Ury, *Getting to YES: Negotiating Agreement Without Giving In*, Penguin, 1981.

Fortune, Dec. 17, 1990, p. 124.

Graham, J.L., and Y. Sano, *Smart Bargaining: Doing Business With the Japanese*, Ballinger, 1984.

Kanter, Rosabeth Moss, *When Giants Learn to Dance*, Merrill, 1989.

Ohmae, K., *The Borderless World: Power and Strategy in the Interlinked Economy*, Harper Business, 1990.

Ouchi, W., *Theory Z*, Addison-Wesley, 1981.

Rubin, J.Z., and B.R. Brown, *The Social Psychology of Bargaining and Negotiation*, Academic Press, 1975.

PART IV
Practical Applications

Successful management starts with the "big picture," but once this is in place, delegation of details to the specialists begins. Thus, marketing experts deal with marketing issues, production engineers manage production, and so on. In this last part of the book, we leave the "big picture" and move to more concrete and technical analysis of some of the functional fields, within the context of "going it alone" in a global market.

Plenert in Chapter 9 and Bensaou in Chapter 10 explore the issues of the transfer and management of production across borders. These chapters provide a direct application of international sourcing, which is in itself an application of the Comparative Cost Model.

If a small or midsize U.S. firm is planning to take advantage of its firm's specific factor by joining with a pool of cheap labor across the border, it must be ready to deal with issues of strategic human resource management. Some examples are presented in Chapter 11, where Teagarden, Butler, and Von Glinow discuss the problems and opportunities of the maquiladora *firms.*

Issues of small and midsize firms exist outside the United States as well. In the re-emerging economies of Eastern Europe, where major corporations were state owned, the success of small firms is of special importance. Mann discusses the experiences and future of small and midsize companies in the economic restructuring of Hungary in Chapter 12. In a book that explores the potential of small and midsize U.S. firms to become global competitors, this chapter provides a comparative look at how the same issues need to be treated outside the United States. It is important to note that even the new managers of Eastern Europe are striving to develop management structures that will allow them to succeed in today's international competition.

9

The Transfer
of Production Planning
and Control Systems from
Plants in the United States
to Other Parts of the World

GERHARD PLENERT

United States managers frequently assume that if they have a production planning and control system that works well in a domestic plant, then this same systems technology will be optimal in a similar plant located in another country. This assumption is the first of several that must be discarded by American companies thinking about overseas expansion. Some others are:

- The basic goals of nations, cultures, and peoples throughout the world are financial, and a pay raise or monetary bonus can motivate any employee.
- The goals of a corporation, as outlined in the business plan, can be accomplished by involving only one or two divisions, such as marketing and finance.
- The United States knows how to do things best, and all other parts of the world should be excited to receive their share of American wisdom, especially when it comes to running factories.
- More data mean more information, which is good.

A research project currently being conducted by the Productivity and Quality Research Group of Brigham Young University in the United States and Chukoy University in Japan focuses on defining, if possible, a world manufacturing management and control model, based on studies of the United States, Europe, Japan, and a number of developing countries. The analysis started with the assumptions under which managers operate, moved to the goals of manufacturing in a variety of environments, and reviewed the operational resource plans. What follows is a summary of this research.

Throw Out the Assumptions

There is a reference at the end of this chapter to my book on why the assumptions are wrong. Here, briefly, is part of the rationale.

(a) There is no one best manufacturing system for all manufacturing environments in all cultures. EOQ (Economic Order Quantity) is not the best. Neither is MRP (Material Requirements Planning) nor MRP II (Manufacturing Resource Planning). The new fads, JIT (Just in Time) and TQM (Total Quality Management), cannot eliminate the competition. A match must be made among the organizational goals, the resource optimized, and the production planning and control system.

(b) Organizational goals vary dramatically between countries. An emphasis on financial goals, such as increased sales, increased profits, return on investments (ROI), return on assets (ROA), reduced costs, and so on, seems to exist primarily in the United States, Canada, and Europe.

(c) Operational goals are frequently out of sync with strategic goals, as expressed in the business plan. When we asked various levels of management to name the goals of the corporation, we often received conflicting answers. No one communicated the organizational goals to operations, so they established their own sets of goals based on the measurement systems in place—assuming that the measurements must be directed toward goal achievement. Managers at the strategic level often fail to realize that goals like increased sales and increased profits may be in direct conflict with each other from an operational perspective.

(d) The United States model for manufacturing, MRP, is appropriate for many industries, but it is not the only way, nor is it the best way for all industries. The same with JIT and TQM. American systems often fail miserably in other countries, not because they are bad systems, but because they are applied inappropriately.

(e) Data can be a curse as well as a blessing. For example, MRP from the United States requires 90 to 95 percent data accuracy and extensive computer power. JIT from Japan, which is better in some areas of manufacturing, collects very little data and needs no computer for production planning and control. Since employees focus on what is being measured, indiscriminate data collection often sends the wrong signals and may therefore be counterproductive. Besides, it wastes time and money.

So Which System Is Best?

In order to compare manufacturing systems, we need to understand why they are different. I will illustrate with three different production-planning philosophies: MRP (Material Requirements Planning), JIT (Just In Time), and OPT (Optimized Production Technology).

Manufacturing lives in a world of three resources, materials, machinery, and labor, with everything else buried in overhead and allocated. A production planning and control system focuses on one of these three resources and attempts to optimize it. MRP uses routings to track labor standards and job sheets to track labor performance, which results in a labor efficiency report. MRP emphasizes labor efficiency at the expense of the other two resources, materials and machinery. In other words, to keep the employees working efficiently, MRP stockpiles inventory in front of each work center and schedules plenty of machine capacity.

With JIT, materials become the resource optimized. Ideally, static work-in-progress should be zero, even at the cost of labor inefficiency and safety capacity in the machine area.

OPT optimizes the bottleneck machine, making it as efficient as possible. Materials efficiency is sacrificed by building up inventory in front of the bottleneck, and labor efficiency by having safety capacity in the nonbottlenecks.

Attempting to optimize more than one resource results in an averaging process that optimizes nothing. The best manufacturing system is the one that optimizes the resource most important to your plant. But, as noted earlier, the selection of a resource to optimize should be based on the goals of the organization. So although there is no globally best production planning and control system, there may be one best system for a particular set of goals and resources. To choose the best system, then, we need to look at the assumptions, goals, and resource focus of a particular factory.

What About the Goals?

Financial goals are the least frequent choices in the world outside the United States. Employee-based goals occur far more often. In Japan, for example, the longevity and security of the employees is often (but not always) the basic goal of the corporation. To achieve this goal, the company strives to dominate its market, assuming that if no competitor can beat it out, its survival is assured.

When I claim that most organizations are not run to meet financial goals, I often hear the rebuttal, "Doesn't a company have to make money in order to survive?" Yes—but a corporation with financial goals also has to consider the needs of employees, or it will not survive. Both factors are necessary for long-term health.

Regardless of whether the primary goal is financial or employee oriented, the company must have secondary goals in areas such as:

- Financial Measures
  High Net Profit
  Increased Sales
  Low Operating Expenses
  Increased Return on Investment (ROI)
  Stable Cash Flow
  Improved Financial Ratios
- Operational Measures
  High Throughput
  Low Inventory
  High Quality
  Increased Market Share
- Other Goals (some influenced by government regulations)
  Vertical Integration
  Stable Production Flow
  Full Employment
  Technology Independence
  Increased Exports
  Improved Balance of Trade

The company must choose which goals to emphasize, primarily because many of them are conflicting. For example, the first two present an operational conflict that most factories encounter. During the first three or three and a half weeks of the month, the plant focuses on efficiency (increased profits). However, to achieve increased sales goals, efficiency is thrown to the winds in the last few days of the month in order to expedite product out the door. Profit is destroyed to increase sales.

A specific goal needs to be clearly defined. The resource planning—and then the production planning and control system—must be built around this goal. All divisions of the corporation, including operations, must have representatives involved in the goal formulation to assure that the plans are operationally feasible.

Which Resource?

Let us suppose that our goal is either reduced costs or increased profits. Our next step would be to examine the value-added cost components that make up our products. The breakdown for a typical United States repetitive discrete manufacturer might look something like this:

Labor Costs	6 to 12 percent
Materials Costs	30 to 40 percent
Overhead	40 to 60 percent

All too often, the most critical resource turns out to be overhead—which means that the manufacturer has no idea what the critical resource really is. In aluminum processing, for example, energy can be a 70 to 80 percent value-added cost component, and energy costs would be buried in overhead.

What I find alarming, however, is that most of the repetitive discrete manufacturers in the United States are running their plants using labor optimization production control systems like MRP when the labor resource is less than 10 percent of the value-added cost components. A more complete list of resources, any of which could be critical, would be:

Material	Plant Location
Labor	Infrastructure
Machinery	Education Levels
Energy	Economic Potential
Maintenance	Automation Level
Vendors	Resource Dependence
Customers	Management Style
Unions	Culture
Government	Environment

An appropriate production planning and control system for the true critical resource may not exist and may need to be developed. For example, if energy is selected as the resource to be optimized, MRP can be stripped of its routings and fitted with a "bill of energy."

The Key Destructive Force

One issue repeatedly emerges from the study of technology transfer of production systems from the United States to other parts of the world—

the problem of conflicting goals. For example, American businesses often emphasize financial goals without regard for their employees' personal goals, which tend to be job security and financial reward. If the corporate goal is increased profits or reduced costs, the employees are treated as a cost that needs to be kept lean—as few and as cheap as possible. So there is a direct conflict between corporate goals and employee goals. Some countries, however, such as Japan, have matched the two.

Is it better to have a conflict of goals between the corporation and the employees, the corporation and the government, the corporation and its vendors, and so on, or is it better to try to harmonize goals between the different parties? Most cultures of the world are moving toward goal harmony, which comes from a different selection of corporate goals than we in the United States are accustomed to.

Summary

What have we learned about the transfer of production planning and control systems from plants in the United States to other parts of the world? First, we learned that many of our *assumptions* about which system is best and who knows the best systems are wrong and need to be changed. Next, we learned that our *goals* are often not the same as those of the culture we are moving to. We may need to find goals that are in harmony with those of the employees, the government, and the culture.

Then we need to analyze our *resource* base to determine which resource is critical in helping us achieve our goal. We build our production planning and control system around this resource. It is important that our *measurement* (data collection) systems focus on this resource. We should not be collecting irrelevant data, because we do not want the employees to get any misconceptions about what is important.

Building a production system that supports the basic goals of the organization does not guarantee success, but it does guarantee focus. And unless we focus properly on our objective, achieving it becomes far more difficult than it needs to be.

REFERENCES

Plenert, Gerhard J., *International Management and Production: Survival Techniques for Corporate America*, Blue Ridge Summit, Penn.: Tap Professional and Reference Books, 1990.

———, "Production Considerations for Developing Countries," *International Journal of Management*, Dec. 1988.

———, "The Development of a Production System in Mexico," *Interfaces*, Vol. 20, No. 3, May–June 1990.

10

Buyer-Supplier Coordination in the United States and Japanese Automobile Industries

BEN M. BENSAOU

In response to the new strategic challenges of global competition, many firms are undergoing profound organizational transformations. Typically, they are streamlining operations and moving toward more external contracting, producing a high level of interdependence between a focal firm and its network. But managers still have little understanding of the new organizational, managerial, and technological skills necessary for the effective coordination of these networks. The buyer-supplier relationships in the U.S. and Japanese automobile industries are examples of this phenomenon, and an examination of the differences between the two countries provides important insights into the factors that contribute to effective performance.

This chapter is based on the responses of a representative sample of 447 managers from automobile firms in the United States and Japan. The questionnaires, which were administered in English and Japanese, were collected and analyzed in the summer of 1991. The results show that automotive buyer-supplier relations in the United States and Japan operate under very different sets of conditions.

Traditionally, U.S. automakers designed the car, manufactured nearly all the necessary core components, and handled final production. The trend, however, is toward a car company's functioning as the coordinator of an intricate production network, with suppliers playing an increasingly important role. Again traditionally, a large number of suppliers would compete for short-term contracts on the basis of price. But the trend is toward longer-term contracts, cooperation to ensure that problems of financing, design, quality, delivery, and cost are tackled at the earliest opportunity, and competition among a small number of suppliers based upon quality, delivery, and engineering capabilities, as well as price.

United States component markets exhibit greater instability and lower concentration of sales than component markets in Japan. This seems to indicate that the U.S. market still operates under traditional mechanisms, where manufacturers spread their business among multiple suppliers selected from a large pool. In contrast, there is higher market stability in the Japanese supply industry. The same few suppliers compete in the same market segments and deliver a much broader range of parts to the manufacturer (see Figure 10.2). And in spite of their larger number of suppliers (and purchasing staff), U.S. manufacturers are still producing internally a greater proportion of a given automobile's parts. Interviews with U.S. suppliers reveal that "the Big Three still want to keep us in competition with their allied [internal] divisions. . . ."

Japanese manufacturers design and produce fewer components. They maintain only a few potential suppliers who have the design and manufacturing skills and capabilities to produce a wide range of parts. These two to three suppliers are perpetually competing in the areas of technology development and improvements in process, product, quality, and cost.

Japanese manufacturers' strategy is to concentrate on their core competencies, to control internally the design and manufacture of the key concepts, technologies, and systems that distinguish them from competitors, but to rely on an elaborate structure of suppliers for much of the rest. The suppliers on the first tier of the structure, generally larger companies, assemble and deliver large integrated systems and carry much of the responsibility for the coordination of suppliers on the second and third tiers. This pyramid permits, as M. S. Flynn and D. J. Andrea described it, "a form of vertical coordination within the industry that simultaneously provides the manufacturer benefits that are traditionally associated with high levels of vertical integration, such as control of the production process, profit opportunity, and protection of their technical core, and those associated with low degrees of vertical integration, such as low cost and a high degree of independence."

The characteristics of the buyer-supplier relationships reflect the differences in the market conditions. Since Japanese manufacturers have fewer choices, they perceive themselves as more dependent on a

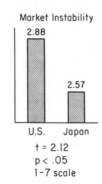

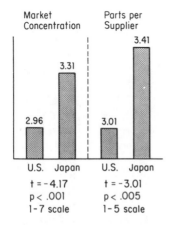 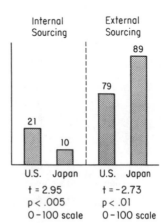

Figure 10.1 Characteristics of the market for components.

specific supplier than U.S. firms do. Indeed, faced with larger, more unstable, and competitive component markets, U.S. manufacturers can keep their switching costs and dependence on suppliers low. In both countries, however, the component suppliers (generally smaller firms) are highly dependent on the revenues brought by the auto company's business.

Surprisingly, U.S. managers are more likely to feel they are making important investments in their relationships with suppliers than their

	Suppliers	Purchasing Staff	Vehicles Built
GM in U.S.	2,500	4,000	5.1 million
Ford in U.S.	1,800	2,200	3.6 million
Toyota in Japan	340	185	4.2 million
Nissan in Japan	310	250	2.4 million

Figure 10.2 Automotive purchasing in the 1980s. Source: Lamming (1990); IMVP Research and Estimates.

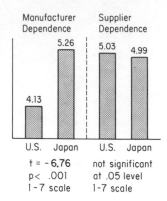

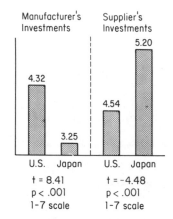

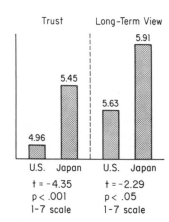

Figure 10.3 Characteristics of the relationship with a supplier.

Japanese counterparts. This may reflect the vision of change affecting attitudes and behaviors in U.S. organizations. But another explanation for lower investments by Japanese manufacturers is, as one told us, "We have spent the last thirty years developing our relationship with our first-tier suppliers and we now let them do much of the design and development of the component. . . . There is little we need to discover about each other any more . . . and we trust they will try hard to keep our business."

Japanese suppliers, on the other hand, are making critical investments in the relationship. U.S. suppliers, despite their high dependence on auto companies, seem to avoid tying assets and investments to any one manufacturer, thus protecting their chances to get business with other domestic firms or the Japanese transplants.

The high level of interdependence in Japanese manufacturer-supplier relationships seems to foster higher mutual trust and a stronger predisposition to continue the relationship in the future. On average,

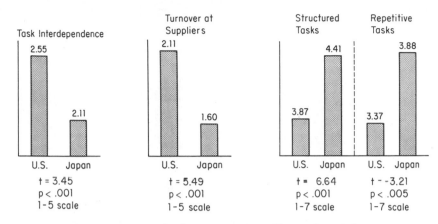

Figure 10.4 Task characteristics of boundary roles.

Japanese relationships have a longer past history (see Figure 10.4). In fact, follow-up interviews with U.S. suppliers revealed that while the relationships might date back for a long time, they were highly inconsistent and intermittent, with little assurance for renewal of the contract.

The tasks of the boundary roles, such as purchasing and engineering, differ sharply between the two countries. United States purchasing managers and engineers spend more time working with a given supplier (in meetings, on the telephone, and so on). The higher turnover rate of personnel among U.S. suppliers may explain the need for more interaction. Boundary roles in Japan tend to be more routine and structured. Japanese managers attributed the difference to "the trust that exists between us and the supplier, the high level of information and knowledge exchange over the years . . . early involvement of the supplier in the design and development of the component." In contrast, U.S. purchasing managers complained they "spent too much of their time trying to get suppliers up to speed and putting out fires at their factories."

Structure for Coordination

Four dimensions of the coordinating structure of the buyer-supplier relationships exhibited significant differences between countries (see Figure 10.5). First, U.S. managers exchange more visits with suppliers, which seems to confirm the efforts that U.S. manufacturers have been making in the last decade to spend more time cultivating the buyer-supplier relationship, moving away from governing it simply through contracts, programs, and procedures. Second, Japanese manufacturers reported working with a greater number of different functional areas with each supplier.

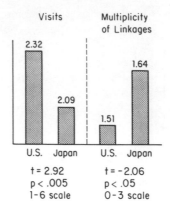

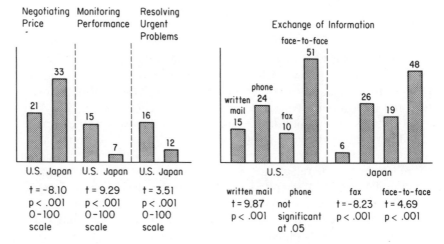

Figure 10.5 Structure for coordination of buyer-supplier relationships.

The third dimension is the time allocated by managers to different tasks during the life cycle of the relationship. United States managers still spend a great part of their time monitoring the performance of the supplier and resolving urgent problems related to production, quality, or delivery issues. Japanese managers, on the other hand, spend comparatively more time in the early stages of the relationship, when they negotiate such things as the division of labor, and design, cost, quality, and delivery requirements. As a result, they spend less time monitoring the supplier. In interviews, Japanese managers related the high performance of their supplier relations to "the early involvement of the supplier in the design and development stages, and the customary practice of exchanging resident engineers during the design phase." Transplant managers also commented that "U.S. firms are starting to make some of the investments [in building the relationship] . . . we also had to make early on with our suppliers. . . . We now waste less time testing each others' intentions."

The choice of media used for the exchange of information, the fourth dimension of the coordinating structure, showed no significant difference in use of the telephone. The use of written mail is comparatively higher in U.S. firms, although low in both countries. Face-to-face interactions are high in both countries, but higher in the United States. The most significant difference appears to be the much greater use of fax machines in Japanese firms.

Interviews revealed the importance in Japan of another distinctive coordinating structure: the formal supplier associations. These associations, organized along the tiered supply pyramid discussed earlier, promote communication and cooperation between the manufacturer and suppliers, and also between suppliers themselves, through annual meetings and study groups involving all levels, from top executives to shop-floor managers. The activities serve to diffuse technical information and product and process innovations.

Information Technology

The pattern and scope of the use of information technology for coordination with suppliers differs greatly between the two countries. While Japanese firms concentrate their investments in a few highly operational areas, such as purchasing and production control, U.S. firms not only rely more on technology altogether, but also apply it to a wider scope of functions (purchasing, engineering, production control, quality, transportation, payment, and so on). Some U.S. information systems managers describe EDI (electronic data interchange) as "the strategic weapon that should allow them to get data from suppliers faster, with less errors and at a lesser cost."

United States firms have established a consortium, the Automotive Industry Action Group (AIAG) to develop industry-wide standards for the electronic exchange of data and documents. The objective is to build an information technology infrastructure for the standard and common use of EDI with all potential suppliers across multiple functional areas. All manufacturers could then coordinate electronically with any supplier and vice versa, eventually creating an electronic market for components. In fact, U.S. firms already exchange electronic data mainly over a network, while Japanese auto firms tend to rely on low-tech solutions (if not using the fax), such as the exchange of magnetic tapes or discs. Also, when Japanese manufacturers do exchange data over existing Value Added Networks (VANs), they tend to impose their proprietary standards onto the suppliers and provide them with less access to their own databases, despite the high level of mutual trust.

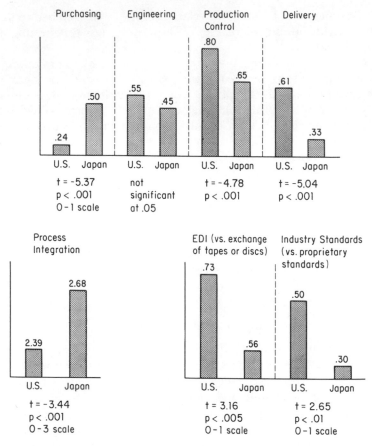

Figure 10.6 Information technology for coordination.

More important, despite a more modest use of information technology across organizational boundaries, Japanese firms achieve greater data and process integration. United States suppliers often need to reenter or convert the data they receive electronically before using it in their internal information systems. A Japanese manager commented, "We are not looking for a quick [technological] fix. . . . It is more important for us to first make sure we have compatible assessment methods and technologies, a common language, and that our scheduling and production processes are well integrated. . . . Once this is accomplished, a tool like the fax can be added to the process if people think we can gain in operational efficiency." He insisted that the main objective is to detect and correct problems as early as in the design process, to integrate the production processes between the two companies, and at the same time to ensure the perfect execution and coordination of processes within each company.

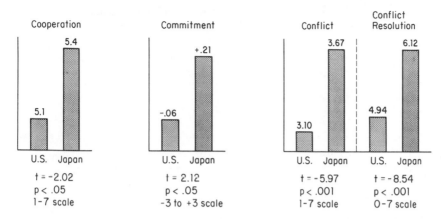

Figure 10.7 Process for coordination or partnership in action.

When we further examined the processes that either fostered or inhibited information exchange between manufacturer and supplier, we were surprised to find that the level of conflict or stress was comparatively higher in Japan (see Figure 10.7). This suggests that the reality is less harmonious than the image and confirms that Japanese manufacturers exert power over suppliers, demanding high levels of quality, tight delivery and inventory schedules, shorter lead times, and expecting them to lower their costs over time. At the same time, however, conflict resolution is much more collaborative in Japanese relationships, as

U.S. firms in the U.S.		
Company/ Division	Number of questionnaires	
	Purchasing	Engineering
A	32	24
B	10	10
C	22	22
D	20	0
Total	84	56

Japanese firms in Japan		
Company	Number of questionnaires	
	Purchasing	Engineering
E	14	0
F	26	24
G	9	16
H	1	1
I	2	2
J	24	24
K	25	25
L	22	23
M	10	10
N	12	13
O	24	0
Total	169	138

Figure 10.8 U.S. firms in the United States/Japanese firms in United States. Breakdown of responses to a survey.

compared with the traditional bargaining and adversarial practices in the United States. In addition, there is more cooperation in Japanese relationships, particularly in areas of joint design and development, together with more commitment (sharing of burdens, risks, and benefits) of manufacturers to the relationship.

Conclusions

The findings from the 447 observations of manufacturer-supplier relationships in the U.S. and Japanese auto industries show two radically different models, each operating under a set of environmental, partnership, and task uncertainties with which firms cope in an internally consistent fashion through a distinctive combination of structure, process, and information technology.

However, the fierce competition and virtual globalization of the auto industry has contributed to the Big Three's recognition of the importance of their suppliers to their own bottom-line cost and quality performance. This has been followed by a variety of programs to promote a new way of doing business, adopting some of the Japanese coordination practices. Nevertheless, the results of our survey, corroborated by interview data, seem to suggest that while U.S. buyer-supplier relationships are effectively changing, the changes are slow and mostly on the surface. Moreover, these changes represent an attempt to blend together elements of two internally consistent, yet inherently different, coordination strategies, and their implementation reflects more a series of reactive business decisions than a clear, coherent strategy.

Suppliers still face short-term price and quality pressures with little assistance and cooperation from the manufacturer, while at the same time they are expected to make immediate investments to achieve cost reduction, quality, and delivery improvements. In fact, they view the increased responsibility (a key assumption in the Japanese model) as another way used by the manufacturer to shift its burden onto them (an interpretation consistent with the traditional U.S. view). It will be no easy matter to convince them that they should change. After all, it took Japanese manufacturers some fifty years of strong commitment and close cooperation to develop smooth and trusting relationships with their now preferred suppliers.

Acknowledgment

The author acknowledges the financial support for this research made available by the Alfred P. Sloan Foundation under the MIT *International Motor Vehicle Program*, the *Management in the 1990s Research Program*, and by the MIT *Center for Information Systems Research (CISR)*. I also thank the managers in the leading firms in the auto industry both in the United

States and Japan for spending time with us and providing the data and interpretations.

REFERENCES

Flynn, M.S., and D.J. Andrea, "Integrated Sourcing: Issues of Dependency, Reliance, and Innovation," University of Michigan, Transportation Research Paper #890233, Society of Automotive Engineers, 1989.

Lamming, R. "The Machine that Changed the World: The Implications for Component Suppliers," Presentation, International Motor Vehicle Program, MIT, 1990.

11

Strategic Human Resource Management in Mexican *Maquiladoras*: The Competitive Edge

MARY B. TEAGARDEN
MARK C. BUTLER
MARY ANN VON GLINOW

One reality of the dynamic, interdependent global economy is that manufacturing costs are higher in some countries than in others. In an effort to seek a competitive edge, firms in industrialized countries frequently look offshore for a way to reduce labor and other factor costs, such as energy or plant and equipment expenses. Historically, the "little dragons"—Taiwan, Singapore, South Korea, and Hong Kong—were the preferred low-cost off-shore manufacturing sites. But as wages and other costs rose in those countries, China, Thailand, Malaysia, Indonesia, and (to a lesser extent) Vietnam became increasingly attractive choices.

While these countries do indeed have low wage rates—the most often cited benefit of off-shore manufacturing—total manufacturing costs are rising, especially when the hidden costs associated with recent and persistent political turbulence in some Pacific Rim countries are included. Many American firms have been finding a better alternative in their own hemisphere.

Mexico's fully fringed wage rates are lower than the little dragons, lower than Brazil, and lower than Spain and Portugal. Since Mexico's population is relatively well educated and the second youngest in the world, the *maquiladora* option is seen by some as a bargain. Comparative wage rate trends, tariff status, political stability, and labor availability in the most common off-shore manufacturing sites are shown in Table 11.1.

Mexico's proximity to U.S. markets and U.S. suppliers is an additional advantage for small and medium-sized U.S. firms who can more closely control, monitor, and interact with their Mexican "off-shore" facilities than with Asian alternatives. Most *maquiladora* sites are less than eight hours from any U.S. city, while Asian sites can require up to a full day's travel time.

Maquilas are especially suitable for the manufacture of mature products with a labor content greater than 30 percent, such as are found in the garment, automotive supply, and electronic assembly industries. A TRW Electronics manager observed that *maquila* production costs can be as much as 50 percent less than those at little dragon sites.

Key management and technical support positions can be staffed with expatriates who often live in the United States and commute to the Mexican border daily. Since many of the hardships associated with an off-shore assignment are avoided, some *maquilas* claim that they can attract better-qualified managers. In addition, costs to the firm of main-

Table 11.1. *Maquila* Industry Activity in 1990

Industry Sector	Border Region		Interior Region	
	Plants	Employees	Plants	Employees
Apparel, Textiles, Footwear & Leather	15.7%	9.0%	29.3%	22.2%
Furniture & Fixtures Wood/Metal Products	14.8%	5.9%	—	—
Transportation Equipment & Accessories	9.8%	21.0%	8.2%	13.6%
Electric & Electronic Machinery, Equipment & Apparatus	7.1%	16.1%	7.5%	13.4%
Electric & Electronic Parts & Accessories	24.5%	26.9%	13.7%	23.6%
Other Manufacturing[a]	23.7%	16.3%	37.3%	24.1%
Service	4.5%	4.7%	3.7%	3.4%

[a]Other Manufacturing includes Food, Chemicals, Toys and Sporting Goods, Non-electrical Equipment, Parts and Apparatus, among other things.

Sources: Instituto Nacional de Estadistica, Geografia e Informatica; *Business Mexico,* March 1990.

taining expatriate families are greatly reduced, since they do not live in a foreign country—they just work there.

Favorable U.S. import laws allow manufacturers using *maquilas* to pay duty only on the value added to the product in Mexico when it returns to the United States, and that is usually determined by the cost of the labor content. Furthermore, Mexico imposes no local content requirement on goods manufactured in *maquilas* that are destined for re-export. *Maquilas* enjoy special treatment under both U.S. Customs regulations and Mexican foreign investment regulations. In 1990, Mexican exports to the United States under U.S. Customs production sharing tariff codes accounted for more than 54 percent of all developing country exports to the United States in this category.

Despite these substantial benefits, *maquiladora* users repeatedly cite difficulties with individual and organizational factors. The most persistent involve international human resource management (IHRM) problems.

The purpose of strategic human resource management (HRM) is to promote overall organizational effectiveness by dovetailing HRM with the firm's business and functional strategies. However, for firms operating internationally, HRM serves other purposes as well. International human resource management practices can enhance the firm's control of its foreign affiliates and act as a mechanism for bridging cross-cultural issues.

Our research of IHRM in *maquiladoras* supports this expanded view. Maximization of benefits associated with *maquiladoras* relies on integration of strategic fit, control, and cross-cultural issues. This integration is best accomplished through IHRM design. Since firms primarily use *maquiladoras* to implement low-cost strategies, IHRM design addresses some of the related issues through reward systems and, to a lesser extent, through interventions such as more effective employee selection methods and training programs.

With these thoughts in mind, we will digress slightly to provide some background information on *maquiladoras*, which is necessary for understanding the special IHRM problems faced by managers there. Then we will identify some specific strategic challenges *maquiladora* managers face and make some recommendations for effective IHRM design.

The Maquiladora "Industry"

Investment in *maquiladoras* is currently growing around 15 percent a year, making this "industry" Mexico's second largest source of hard currency, after petroleum sales. At the beginning of 1991, the total value-added exceeded $1.6 billion (U.S.). More than 487,000 workers

—about two-thirds women between the ages of 16 and 25—were employed in 1,880 plants.

The groundwork began in 1965 when Mexico partially relaxed restrictive foreign investment policies through the Border Industrialization Program (BIP). At that time, the United States had terminated the *bracero* program, which had allowed the seasonal entry of up to 500,000 Mexican workers into the United States, and Mexican officials saw the BIP as a means of providing jobs for the displaced male agricultural workers. The BIP permitted establishment of *maquilas* (the terms *maquilas* and *maquiladoras* are used interchangeably), "off-shore" manufacturing plants for assembly, processing, or finishing of foreign material and components, located in specially designated regions along the U.S.–Mexico border. There was some anticipation that twin plants would be built, with labor-intensive processes carried out on the Mexican side and the rest on the U.S. side, but only about 10 percent of the *maquiladoras* have a U.S. twin. The program also allowed duty-free import of all equipment, machinery, raw materials, and other components needed in production, as long as the resultant products were to be exported.

In October, 1972, the program was expanded to permit establishment of plants in the interior of Mexico (excluding highly industrialized areas such as Mexico City), but less than 20 percent of the *maquilas* are located inland. The program was given a further boost with the devaluation of the peso in 1982, when Mexican labor became one of the least expensive in the world. More recently, however, growth has slowed. In 1989 the Mexican government increased the proportion of *maquila* products that can be sold domestically from 20 percent to 50 percent of total production, but managers complain that it is still difficult to sell *maquila* products in Mexico.

The goals for the BIP today remain the same: to increase Mexico's level of industrialization, especially in the border region; to create new jobs; to raise the domestic income level; to facilitate absorption of technology and skills (technology transfer); and to attract much-needed foreign exchange.

The *maquiladora* "industry" is actually an agglomeration of manufacturers from various industrial sectors, including among others the automotive supply, computer, television and other electronics-based industries, medical supply, woodworking, furniture manufacture, and garment industries. *Maquila* users include both large multinationals such as Ford, Hewlett Packard, and General Motors, and small manufacturing firms. These companies can take advantage of *maquila* benefits through wholly owned subsidiaries, joint ventures, and shelter or subcontracting agreements.

Maquila plant size ranges from more than 1800 employees in some automotive and electronic assembly plants to six- or eight-person job shops in woodworking and garment operations. Mexican officials estimate that about 20 percent of the *maquilas* use robotics in assembly operations that are considered state-of-the-art in their industries. The Sony television *maquilas* and both Ford and General Motors auto supply *maquilas* are examples. Generally, automotive suppliers cluster in the El Paso/Juarez region, while electronics-related industries, woodworking and furniture making, and garment industries cluster in the San Diego/Tijuana region. Table 11.2 shows the industry distribution.

United States investors control the largest number of *maquilas* and account for more than 90 percent of their value. While large firms such as Ford, General Motors, Eastman Kodak, Caterpillar, Hewlett Packard, American Home Products, Johnson & Johnson, and Westinghouse use *maquilas*, more than half are affiliates of small and medium-sized U.S. firms.

Japan is most notable among "third countries" that are increasing their *maquila* presence. Sony, Sanyo, Fujitsu, Matsushita, and Hitachi use *maquilas*, and they are encouraging their suppliers from Japan to follow. Japanese *maquilas* are few in number but large in size, employing about 15 percent of the workers. They are located predominantly in Baja California Norte, close to their U.S. affiliates in California.

Table 11.2.   Mexico's *Maquiladora* Industry 1978–1990

Year	Number of Plants (% Change)		Value Added[a] (% Change)		Number of Employees (% Change)	
1978	457	(—)	452	(—)	90,704	(—)
1979	549	(20.1)	638	(41.2)	115,014	(26.8)
1980	620	(12.9)	772	(21.0)	123,897	(7.7)
1981	610	(−1.6)	976	(26.4)	130,102	(5.0)
1982	588	(−3.7)	832	(−14.7)	122,493	(−5.8)
1983	629	(6.9)	828	(−0.5)	173,128	(41.3)
1984	730	(16.1)	916	(10.6)	208,512	(20.4)
1985	842	(15.3)	1,028	(12.3)	250,000	(19.9)
1986	981	(16.5)	1,181	(14.9)	280,000	(12.0)
1987	1,125	(14.6)	N/A[b]	(—)	305,000	(8.9)
1988	1,490	(32.4)	N/A[b]	(—)	380,000	(24.5)
1989	1,632	(9.5)	1,444	(—)	427,900	(12.6)
1990	1,880	(13.2)	1,590	(10.1)	487,000	(13.8)

[a]US$ millions
[b]Data not available
Sources: Secretariat of Planning and Budget, *Latin American Monitor,* Mexico, 1990; Annual Report on Government, *Economy & Business,* p. 99; Instituto Nacional de Estadistica, Geografia e Informatica; Banco Nacional de Comercio Exterior (BANCOMEXT).

Korean multinationals such as Samsung, Lucky, Goldstar, and Hyundai have recently established *maquilas*, and there are a small number from Germany (whose total foreign direct investment in Mexico surpasses that of Japan), France, Finland, the Netherlands, Canada, and Taiwan.

The largest controversy surrounding *maquila* operations involves workforce utilization issues—especially U.S. workforce displacement and Mexican workers' health and safety. Specifically, U.S. firms have come under fire from organized labor, which has criticized them for taking jobs away from U.S. workers and for exploiting Mexican workers. Some Mexicans also complain that *maquilas* exploit workers through low wages, poor working conditions, and disruption of the traditional Mexican social system. Additionally, some charge that the *maquilas* are not meeting their original purpose of employing displaced male agricultural workers.

Japanese *maquilas*—which are formed by the U.S. affiliates of the Japanese multinationals to take advantage of the favorable trade laws designed to benefit U.S. firms—have also come under fire for taking jobs away from U.S. workers. Studies from Wharton, however, concluded that use of *maquilas* by U.S. corporations (with either U.S. or Japanese parents) has an almost negligible effect on U.S. employment that is in fact slightly positive. (Keep in mind that research indicates that the alternative for U.S. manufacturers who choose *maquilas* is an off-shore site in the Pacific Rim or the Caribbean, *not* relocation or automation in the United States.) *Maquilas* do, of course, create displacement—jobs are lost in Detroit and St. Louis and created in San Diego and El Paso. More than that, it is lower-skilled U.S. jobs that are lost, while semi-skilled and skilled U.S. jobs are created.

Strategic IHRM Challenges in Maquiladoras

Labor costs are a function of both the hourly wage rate and worker productivity or output. Since "cheap Mexican labor" is a primary *maquila* benefit—and since IHRM specifically targets the productivity side of the equation—strategic IHRM issues acquire a special importance. The IHRM-based strategic challenges in *maquilas* include a youthful workforce of "green hands," workers without previous manufacturing exposure or meaningful work experience, often from rural Mexico; significant cross-cultural differences; abundant unskilled labor; labor law influences that commonly favor the worker; and family management issues that spill over to the workplace.

Although most *maquilas* are located along the U.S.–Mexico border, many workers have migrated there from the interior, frequently within the last five years, and have no local family. Two-thirds of the *maquila* assembly workers are women between the ages of 16 and 25 (16 is the average age of the Mexican population) with little manufacturing-related work experience. Most workers have six to nine years of education.

Maquila employers, especially in electronic manufacturing, explain that young women are best suited to assembly processes requiring high levels of fine motor skills, that women are better suited to the tedious work, and that they are more stable than men. They also put forth a culturally based argument, that the assembly jobs are not seen as sufficiently *macho*, and thus are shunned by men. Some researchers have countered that young women are hired because they are docile, compliant, and hard to unionize.

Gender-related *maquila* employment trends are changing, however. The employment of men is increasing, from 15 percent of the workforce in 1965 to 44 percent in 1990. Men are more prevalent in woodworking and furniture manufacturing, leather processing, and automotive supply. Nevertheless, men are often perceived to be using *maquila* employment as a stopover on their way north. Sanoh's personnel manager asks prospective male employees how many times they have crossed the border. If they have done it and been sent back two or three times, he figures it is a good time to hire them.

Machismo, a trait closely associated with Latin American men that is characterized by pride, reluctance to admit error or ignorance, and an unwillingness to do "women's work," is found not just among workers but in local supervisors as well, as the following example from an article by M. E. DeForest in *Automotive Industries* indicates:

> Recently, an American manager of a Mexican *maquiladora* producing automotive parts was proud that his final inspection reports received 98% or 99% quality ratings. However, he was puzzled. Production efficiencies were low and raw-material costs inexplicably high. . . . Determined to find out why, he was aghast to learn that the supervisors [all male] secretly threw out the bad pieces every night. He was unaware that the Mexican supervisors were too proud to "confess" they did not know how to adjust the malfunctioning equipment. So they chose to discard bad pieces.

The importance of family and the family structure to Mexican workers is also a significant cross-cultural difference. As Oscar Lewis commented, "Without his family, the Mexican individual stands prey to every form of aggression, exploitation, and humiliation." Mexicans value an extended kinship system in which relatives, clans, and organizations are expected to look after, and care for, the individual. In exchange, the individual owes absolute allegiance.

Thus, paternalism is expected in *maquilas*—the appropriate role of management is to take care of the workers. Managers and supervisors are expected to be the authorities. Their status is respected, but in return the worker's status is also to be respected. From this perspective, workers are the manager's "extended family"—the manager is the *patron*. When asked what they would change if they were supervisors, *maquila* assembly workers' responses included encouraging workers to share problems so that supervisors could make necessary or appropriate changes to solve them; helping the workers actually do their jobs; creating a more sociable work environment; holding social events; not making workers nervous; and allowing workers to work at their own pace.

Maquilas have the right to determine staffing needs and to recruit and fire personnel on their own (unlike, for example, the People's Republic of China, where staffing can require absorption of an unwieldy number of excess employees). Union influence is strong in some regions, especially the eastern Mexican border, but the influence is seen by most employers as having a positive effect: Unions tend not to be militant, and they supply a pool of readily available labor. According to one employer, "We announce fifty openings on Friday, and by Monday we have five hundred applicants." Of course, some of them jump from other *maquilas* to shorten a commute or to get marginally better working conditions.

The abundance of applicants allows employers to screen for and select those most suitable for assembly jobs. *Maquilas* do, however, have a difficult time recruiting skilled labor. Managers with effective operations engage in extensive, and often costly, training in order to assure minimum levels of competence.

Mexico has strong labor laws that influence HRM practices, although anecdotal evidence suggests that the laws are not evenly enforced. Laws specify vacations and holidays, acceptable reasons for termination, provisions for pregnant and nursing mothers, seniority premium pay, and so on. Minimum wages vary by region and employment classification. The work week is 48 hours, but many *maquila* employees work five nine-hour days and are paid for 48 hours. Benefits such as holiday pay, meals, housing, child care, and production incentives can boost wages 30 to 100 percent above the minimum wage, although many of these benefits are optional. One week of vacation after the first year of employment is required, increasing at two days per year until two weeks of vacation are reached. A 25 percent premium is paid on vacation pay.

When a new worker is hired, the employer has four weeks to evaluate performance, then the worker is "permanent." Since Mexico does not have a fire-at-will doctrine, termination can be costly. Permanent workers receive severance pay, and *maquila* managers say that some only work until they build up enough to see them through the rest of the year before leaving.

In fact, workers commonly leave on vacation or for the Christmas holidays and fail to return to work as scheduled, usually for "family reasons." "Family reasons" are also the most common excuses for absenteeism and turnover. They include, among other things, the need to take care of small children, sick children, brothers and sisters, elderly parents, and other relatives. If the worker's family is in the interior, he or she may have to return home to resolve the problem. Since family is very important to the Mexican worker, as we mentioned earlier, "family reasons" is a legitimate excuse for absence.

Some *maquilas* face turnover approaching 30 percent per month and very high absenteeism—factors that greatly increase labor costs. Many managers lament that *maquila* workers simply "work to live" and are not committed to their jobs. Nevertheless, *maquila* workers remain among the lowest-cost labor in the world, and some firms have made effective use of the *maquila* option. IHRM responses to the challenges are at the heart of their successes.

Recruitment, Selection, and Training

When turnover runs above 30 percent, one cause is ineffective recruitment policies. Employees of *maquilas* are commonly recruited by word-of-mouth—especially through workers seeking employment for family members—or by signs hung outside the door. The purpose of choosing a recruitment strategy is to generate qualified labor in sufficient numbers to assure selection of an effective workforce, which in this case includes stabilizing what can be dramatic fluctuations. One possible strategy would be to take the money budgeted for advertising job openings on public media and give it as bonuses to employees who recruit others.

Prospective employees are interviewed in Spanish, and a limited number go through additional screening. Although the evidence is anecdotal, *maquilas* using extensive screening processes—physical examinations, intelligence, and dexterity tests—report lower turnover rates than industry averages. Workers who score well on intelligence tests, but not on dexterity tests, are often channeled into clerical and administrative positions. But since many of the young female employees only work until they start a family, and many male employees see *maquilas* only as a stopover on their way north, retention remains a problem.

Because most entry-level workers lack experience in a manufacturing environment, and many are from the agrarian interior of Mexico, on-the-job training is necessary to help them develop important social skills. Initial orientation stresses basics such as punctuality and regular attendance. Quality control and quality circles are common training topics in the electronics and automotive industries; welding and soldering training are also common in electronics. Many *maquila* workers consider training a desired reward.

In addition to job-related training, some employers offer on-site general education courses to target the needs of workers who are removed from their familiar social environment and who have a tendency to bring their personal problems to the workplace. These courses include budgeting family finances and basic health-care practices. Companies such as Ford and Sony have invested heavily in additional training for key technical personnel, often sending *maquila* workers to manufacturing facilities in the United States or Japan. Though, again, the reports are anecdotal, *maquilas* that offer both job-related and general training claim lower turnover rates and higher productivity than industry averages.

Reward Systems and Appraisal

While wages are higher in *maquilas* than in other Mexican manufacturing plants, there is considerable pressure from the others to keep *maquila* wages low. Consequently, perquisites are used to increase the compensation package. Allen Bradley, Pulse Engineering, and Sanyo are among those offering perquisite combinations that may include transportation from central urban and rural locations to the plant; employee funds that build up based on hours worked and are distributed on a scheduled basis; quality and punctuality bonuses; on-site health-care clinics for workers and their families; cafeterias that serve traditional Mexican food, often free; free beverage dispensers; shower facilities; on-site general education; athletic activities; and packages of food and makeup for women workers.

Maquila managers say that the use of such rewards enhances overall effectiveness and helps them maintain lower manufacturing costs. However, there has been little systematic research to explore the IHRM design interventions used or to evaluate the effectiveness of specific mechanisms.

A critical issue here involves tying the rewards to performance. Every time a "reward" is given for something other than performance—for example, a punctuality bonus for simply showing up—the employee has one less reason to perform. Our observations indicate that worker expectations about the roles of employer and employee have a strong influence here: *maquila* workers perform because the employer is providing *expected* entitlements, and thus filling the role of *patron*. Nevertheless, performance is higher when rewards are directly tied to quality and output performance targets.

The dominant function of appraisal in *maquilas* is traditional. That is, for internal promotion purposes, the systems track those individuals with the greatest demonstrated ability to supervise the efforts of other *maquila* workers and those individuals who simply perform adequately on the job. However, in light of the high turnover rate, the appraisal setting provides a strategic opportunity for the supervisor and the employee to engage in a number of developmental activities. This is espe-

Table 11.3. Off-Shore Manufacturing Site Benefit Profiles

	Average industrial monthly wage			Duty status	Political risk	Available labor
	1984	1988	Change			
South Korea	$302	$633	+110%	MFN[a]	Some	Shortages
Taiwan	$325	$598	+84%	MFN	Slight	Shortages
Hong Kong	$363	$544	+50%	MFN	Medium	Shortages
Singapore	$416	$547	+32%	MFN	Slight	Shortages
PRC	$53	$76	+43%	GSP[b]	High	Abundant
Mexico	$144	$109	−24%	GSP	Slight	Abundant

[a]MFN = Goods imported from countries with Most Favored Nation status are charged duties averaging 5 to 10% based on product classification.

[b]GSP = Goods imported are exempt from duties under the General System of Preference.

cially true since the loyalty *maquila* workers feel toward the firm is strongly influenced by their attitude toward their immediate supervisor.

Content analysis of open-ended responses to surveys administered in *maquilas* showed clearly that the typical Mexican worker chronically complained that supervisors and managers did not view them as people or as individuals, only as workers. Those feelings can be dispelled, or at least modified, in a performance appraisal. Given the limited ability of most *maquilas* to offer wage incentives, and the increasing level of competition for workers, altering simple procedures like performance appraisals to appeal to the needs of the employee can produce significant gains in effectiveness.

Family and Career Issues

Problems associated with the management of family issues have perhaps the most insidious influence on *maquila* effectiveness. As stated, family issues are the most cited reason for both turnover and absenteeism. Some effective ways of addressing these issues are providing on-site health-care facilities for workers and their families, developing or coordinating childcare facilities, or making small loans to workers to help them through financially troubled times. Although these options contribute to the overall cost of labor, the firms using them feel that they are more attractive employers as a result and that the benefits of stabilizing the workforce outweigh the costs of the programs.

Given the instability of the industry, it is tempting to shrug off career issues. But many workers we have surveyed state clearly that their principle interest is in a career advancement opportunity. In particular, a group of workers we interviewed and surveyed in the Tijuana/San Diego area indicated their preference for learning more about what their American counterparts did on the job *even if that meant forgoing salary or wage increases.* And the industry is beginning to stabilize. For example, in the Tijuana/San Diego area, the rapid growth seen over the past decade, which reached as high as 30 percent per year, has slowed to between 16 and 18 percent per year. This figure should remain steady, or decline only slightly, over the next several years, even with full implementation of the North American Free Trade Agreement (NAFTA). In order to remain competitive, organizations should begin now to invest in career development for their workers, thus creating opportunities and building incentives for longer-term commitments.

Spillover Benefits of Strategic IHRM

Effective IHRM design has implications beyond the firms adopting it. To the degree that culturally appropriate and effective HRM systems can be developed and implemented in *maquilas*, Mexico is the recipient of valuable "soft" technology—HRM technology—that spills over to other *maquilas* and thence to domestic industry. And effective HRM practices make *maquilas* increasingly attractive off-shore manufacturing sites, thus also increasing the likelihood of higher levels of direct foreign investment. In addition, firms are willing to transfer more technology-intensive manufacturing processes to effective affiliates. These technology-intensive manufacturing processes will also spill over to domestic industry.

The firms themselves benefit by enhancing the benefits of the *maquila* off-shore option: low labor and other factor costs; proximity to the U.S. market and suppliers, and thus low transportation costs; easier control because of the proximity to the parent firm; and preferential treatment on reimported products. For "third country" users, *maquilas* offer quasi-insider status in U.S. markets, since they benefit from the same laws as U.S. firms do. For example, Japanese *maquila* products are not counted against Japanese import quotas.

As the 1990s unfold, and NAFTA is implemented, both U.S.- and Canadian-based manufacturers will gain increased access not only to Mexican labor, but to a market of 86 million potential consumers, 20 million of whom currently have the buying power of average U.S. consumers. The envisioned region created by NAFTA will be more populous that the European Community (EC) and not far behind the EC in industrial output and gross national product. Mexican and U.S. officials assure manufacturers that *maquilas* will continue to receive preferential treatment on both sides of the border. *Maquilas* therefore represent an excellent expansion opportunity for U.S. and Canadian-based firms that plan to take advantage of NAFTA benefits.

Finally, there are benefits from effective *maquila* use that have implications for the firm's long-term global competitiveness. Effective management of a *maquila* requires the ability to meet the challenges of cultural—and hence global—diversity. Thus, as firms learn to be effective *maquila* managers, they also learn how to be effective managers of global diversity. Other cultures and contexts the firm faces may very well be different, but the processes used to manage effectively in the face of diversity are the same. Ultimately, the firms that learn to best leverage their human assets will be the firms that gain the competitive edge and win the global competitiveness challenge.

REFERENCES

DeForest, M.E., "Managing a Maquiladora," *Automotive Industries*, May 1989.

Godshaw, G., C. Pinon-Farah, M. Pinon-Farah, G. Schink, V. Singh, "The Implications for the U.S. Economy of Tariff Schedule Item 807 and Mexico's Maquila Program," The Wharton Econometric Group, 1988.

Lewis, Oscar, *Five Families: Mexican Case Studies in the Culture of Poverty,* Basic Books, 1959.

12

Small and Midsize Enterprises in the United States and East-Central Europe: Common Challenges in the 1990s

CATHERINE L. MANN

The proposition that small to midsize enterprises in one of the largest industrial market economies and those in countries making the transition to a market economy have something in common does not seem likely at first glance. Moreover, the notion that successful performance of these firms is the key to domestic economic growth also seems far-fetched. However, there are several interesting parallels.

First, competitive small and midsize firms would facilitate needed structural adjustments both in the United States and East-Central Europe (ECE). In the United States, as small and midsize firms respond vigorously to external trade opportunities, employment, production, income, and savings can expand, even in times of domestic recession. In ECE, an expanding private small and midsize sector can support growth, increase income, reduce inflation, and aid the transition of production and labor away from large state-owned enterprises (SOEs).

Second, small and midsize firms often lead innovation and productivity. The productivity slowdown in the United States and other industrial countries is well documented and has contributed to lackluster competitiveness. A more robust small and midsize enterprise (SME) sector focused on external competition could reverse this trend. In ECE, years of irrational industry structure contributed to growth well below potential. Moreover, absorption of existing technology has been slower than in economies with healthy private sectors. An expanding SME sector would be the most likely source of technology and innovation in ECE, through both internal research and development and foreign joint ventures.

Third, midsize firms in the two marketplaces face surprisingly similar challenges, although these are clearly more apparent and pressing in ECE. Access to credit is often biased against SMEs. In ECE, the current state of the financial system puts SME borrowers at a particular disadvantage. SMEs can have greater difficulty breaking into established input and distribution networks. In ECE, some of these channels are poorly developed and some monopolized. Information on domestic and foreign market opportunities is often difficult for SMEs to obtain and act on. In ECE, business service sector information networks are only now being revived. Finally, tapping foreign markets compounds these problems with exchange risk, different regulations, and the need to find foreign marketing representatives. In ECE, through 1990, one-third or more of trade was arranged between state trading organizations. Trade is only now being redirected to market economies, and private entrepreneurs have only recently been allowed to trade in international markets.

The government challenge is to level the playing field for midsize business without reducing the incentives to compete. Intervening to eliminate the rough spots for this group recognizes that the market may undervalue the economy-wide benefits of a vibrant SME sector. In addition, the ECE economic structure was historically inimical to SMEs, and incomplete economic reforms have barely reduced the distinct bias against SMEs. Current government response bears some relationship to the types of policies employed in the United States to encourage SMEs: preferential credit, antitrust and competition policies, business advisory services, and export-import services. However, after a history of disallowing private enterprise in favor of centralized production and distribution, ECE governments had to begin by legislating the very existence of the SME sector.

Realizing that performance of SMEs is important both for the United States and ECE, and that the situation is far more critical in ECE, I would like to focus particularly on the challenges, policies, and performance of SMEs in Hungary, including the opportunities for foreign direct investment and joint ventures there.

SMEs in Market Economies and in ECE

The development of the SME sector is a key underpinning for the transition to a market economy. As manufacturers, SMEs in industrial market economies produce intermediate inputs and final goods for market niches that increase the flexibility and efficiency of overall production and add to the diversity of goods available. As distributors and wholesalers in internal and external trade, SMEs link the larger firms to each other and to the final consumers. As the competitive core of the economy, they channel and refine the price signals between producers and consumers.

Figure 12.1 shows a stylized version of a market economy with large producers, small consumers, and a vibrant SME sector of smaller manufacturers, distributors, and retailers. These roles are particularly important in the transition to a market economy from one where relative prices were fixed and irrational for many years and where the forces of supply and demand were consistently muted.

There is no precise definition for midsize enterprises. They are somewhere between the atomistic entrepreneur and the large corporation in terms of complexity, number of employees, and economic power.

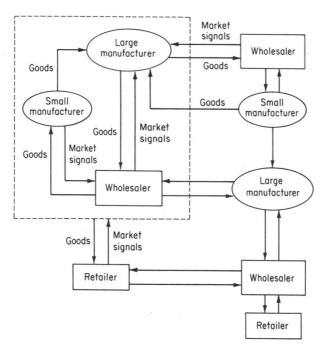

Figure 12.1 Stylized representation of the manufacturing sector in a market economy.

The midsize manufacturing enterprise has greater fixed investment and working capital requirements, greater demand for organized labor input (as in a team or on a production line), and requires more management than an entrepreneurship, but is too small to wield economic power over input or output markets. Such an enterprise could be a subsidiary of a large corporation so long as it remains a separate decision-making unit. Generally, midsize firms can be considered those with between 100 and 500 employees, although different products and different countries will have somewhat different firm size distribution, depending on domestic resources and preferences, lines of corporate financial and managerial control, and production and distribution technology of major industries.

Table 12.1 quantifies the importance of the SME sector for employment, value of manufacturing output, and value of exports in several industrial and industrializing market economies. Small and midsize firms are the core of the economy. More than 85 percent of firms employ fewer than 100 people, although they account for only about one-third of manufacturing employment and about one-fourth of the value of manufacturing output. Midsize firms account for about 10 percent of total firms, and one-third of both employment and output. In all, then, the SME sector accounts for about 95 percent of the number of firms, more than two-thirds of employment, and 60 percent of output.

SMEs are also key players in the manufacturing distribution network. Table 12.2 quantifies the role of wholesalers and retailers of manufactured goods products. The number of wholesalers nearly doubles the population of businesses devoted to the transmission of market signals throughout the economy. The number of retailers per wholesaler ranges from four to twelve (for this group of countries), indicating that reaching the customer in a market economy requires substantial business infrastructure. Moreover, wholesale and retail operations are, on average, small operations.

An increase in the number of small and midsize manufacturing establishments and an expansion of the wholesale and retail network in ECE would increase the complexity of the domestic economy, expand the nodes where the supply and demand determination of market prices takes place, and create a large reservoir of jobs for those being released by the state-owned enterprises.

Clearly, midsize enterprises increase the complexity of linkages throughout the economy. Hence, they are incompatible with central planning, and the legacy of planning is a dearth of midsize enterprises in ECE. The dotted lines in Figure 12.1 denote the boundaries of the stylized state-owned enterprise in ECE under planning. Small-scale manufacturers of inputs or ancillary supplies were drawn into the main production unit. Wholesale and retail trade in the planned economy were particularly circumscribed because their operations, according to the

Table 12.1. The Small and Midsize Manufacturing Sector in Market Economies: Importance for Manufacturing Employment, Output, and Exports

	Small	Medium	Large	Mega
	Size of Establishment			
	(number of employees)			
United States	(1−100)	(100−500)	(500−2500)	(>2500)
% of establishments	90	8	2	<1
% of employment	28	34	24	14
% of output	21	32	31	16
United Kingdom	(1−100)	(100−500)	(500−1000)	(>1000)
% of establishments	95	5	1	<1
% of employment	34	35	13	19
Japan	(4−100)	(100−500)	(500−1000)	(>1000)
% of establishments	97	3	<1	<1
% of employment	56	30	7	14
% of output	34	40	13	26
Korea	(5−100)	(100−500)	(>500)	
% of establishments	91	8	2	
% of employment	33	29	40	
% of output	16	26	57	
Netherlands	(10−100)	(100−500)	(>500)	
% of establishments	86	12	2	
% of employment	32	26	42	
% of output	15	26	59	
% of exports	25	27	48	

Note: Data are for 1982 for the United States; 1988 for the United Kingdom, 1983 for Japan; 1982 for Korea, and 1986 for Netherlands.

Marxist teachings, did not add value to the economy. Accordingly, wholesale trade did not exist at all, and distribution and retail trade were tied directly to the main producer.

Data on the size distribution of firms in Czechoslovakia, Poland, and Hungary (see Table 12.3) shows how the industrial structures of these economies varies from that in the market economies. Czechoslovakia embraced planning and state ownership the most completely, and it has the most centralized manufacturing structure. In Poland, SMEs were more important in the population of enterprises; 57 percent of manufacturing enterprises were small and midsize. But they were not important contributors to employment. While mega enterprises are not unimportant in market economies, accounting for around 20 percent of employ-

Table 12.2. Wholesale and Retail Distribution in Market Economies

	United States	United Kingdom	Japan	Korea
Wholesale per manufacturing establishment	1.16	—	0.96	1.24
Retail outlets per wholesaler	4.62	—	3.94	11.91
Retail outlet per person	0.008	0.006	0.014	0.013
Employees per wholesaler	11.98	—	9.68	3.80
Employees per retail outlet	7.52	6.80	3.98	1.74

Note: Data are for 1982 for United States, 1986 for United Kingdom, 1985 for Japan, and 1982 for Korea.

ment and output, the difference in ECE is that the SME sector, if it exists, has played a very small role in employment and output in comparison to its importance in these two areas in market economies.

Hungary is starting to develop a more diversified manufacturing industrial structure. In an effort to increase productivity, the government began to encourage industrial cooperatives some two decades ago. These are smaller economic units with greater autonomy in economic decision making, although they are still nominally owned by the state. As of 1988, there were about equal numbers of cooperatives and enterprises (1582 and 1143 respectively). The cooperatives have not played as significant a role as have SMEs in market economies: They accounted for only 15 percent of workers and 8 percent of the value of industrial output in 1988. Large state enterprises (greater than 500 employees) were the dominant industrial form, accounting for 18 percent of firms, 83 percent of employment, and 40 percent of output. Even so, the government's loosening of central planning resulted in an industrial sector with a relatively greater diversity of firm size than other ECE countries, and some that have operated in close to a market context.

Before the recent reforms, the wholesale network in Hungary had been incorporated into the production enterprises. The retail network, although principally tied to the state-owned manufacturing enterprise, appears to be relatively well developed. The ratio of retail outlets to manufacturing enterprises in 1988 was 25 to 1, much higher than the comparable statistic in the market economies, but the number of retail outlets per person was 0.006, about on par with the industrial econ-

Table 12.3. The Small and Midsize Manufacturing Sector in East–Central Europe: Importance for Manufacturing Employment and Output

	Size of Enterprise			
Czechoslovakia	*Small & Midsize*	*Large*	*Very Large*	*Mega*
	(1–500)	(500–1000)	(500–2500)	(>2500)
% of enterprises	10	20	45	25
% of employment	2	7	35	56
Poland	*Small*	*Medium*	*Large*	*Mega*
	(1–100)	(100–500)	(500–1000)	(>1000)
% of enterprises	17	50	15	18
% of employment	1	18	15	66
Hungary	*Small*	*Medium*	*Large*	*Mega*
	(1–100)	(100–500)	(500–2000)	(>2000)
% of enterprises				
State-owned	30	29	34	10
Industrial cooperatives	67	31	2	0
Overall manufacturing	50	30	16	4
% of employment				
State owned	1	9	43	47
Industrial cooperatives	23	60	17	0
Overall manufacturing	4	17	39	40
% of output				
State-owned	1	9	39	52
Industrial cooperatives	29	57	13	0
Overall manufacturing	3	13	37	48

Note: Data are for 1988.

omies. This further suggests that what is missing from Hungary (and the other ECE economies) is the numerous small and midsize enteprises.

Creating the Small and Midsize Private Sector

The two interrelated challenges facing ECE governments are to create an SME sector and to create a stable and competitive economic environ-

ment. Trade and related external policies are important for both challenges. As a first step in encouraging the growth and development of an
SME sector, the governments have legalized private enterprise.

Legalizing private ownership of the means of production and legalizing the concept of profit were prerequisites to creation of an SME
sector. Although both were allowed to some degree in most ECE countries before the political revolutions, they were usually limited by the
requirement that the individual or family had to work the capital or land
alone.

In 1989 Hungary eliminated the limits on capital that an individual
could own and the number of employees he or she could hire to produce
output. Additional legal codes introduced or amended in 1990 that were
specifically directed toward private markets were the Business Corporation Act, which provides for several different corporate structures (corporations limited by share, companies with limited liability, joint enterprises), business associations, and partnerships (both general and
limited); and the Securities Act, which applied to all securities bought
and sold through public offerings, thus creating the foundation for the
corporate structure common to industrial market economies.

The second step the Hungarian government is taking to create a
small and midsize business sector is to spin off to private investors
through auction the distribution and retail parts of the large state-owned
enterprises. In fact, the Hungarian government has the ambitious goal of
privatizing half of its holdings of over 90 percent of Hungarian industry
by 1994.

But a market economy cannot be created by merely privatizing
existing enterprises as they are, because the SOEs are not economically
rational conglomerates, and the planned economy lacked complex market linkages. The Hungarian approach merges the two needs of the
market economy (increased linkages and more private entrepreneurs)
by auctioning retail outlets and distribution facilities of the large SOEs
and then leaving additional restructuring of the main production unit to
a private investor group with its own objectives.

Hungary's privatization programs have several unique features.
First, in keeping with the greater diversity in size distribution of firms,
there are separate programs for large, medium, and small enterprises.
Second, Hungary's privatization methods depend more on market
forces, particularly auction bidding, than do those of other governments
in the region. Third, Hungary will compensate owners of expropriated
capital or land with transferable certificates that entitle the holder to
shares in privatized enterprises or that may be used as tender in public
auctions (this is in contrast to restoring property to its original owner).
Finally, Hungary has more avidly courted foreign investors than have
other governments.

The program for small service establishments, retail outlets, and distribution facilities (warehouses and trucks) involves auctioning about two-thirds of the 16,000 state-owned facilities to individuals. The objective is to create a middle class of private business people. An important question is whether the small enterprises thus created will be too fragmented. For example, small retail outlets without access to a variety of new suppliers or an independent distribution network may carry the same goods and act no more independently than when owned by the state. Because there is little business experience, franchising may have merit.

Medium-sized enterprises are being sold via a more transparent version of the 1989 spontaneous privatization method. Any investor (domestic or foreign) can identify a target firm, thus "putting it in play." The State Property Agency (SPA) must respond within 30 days with any conditions on the bid (such as employment contracts). Meanwhile, the firm is transformed into a joint stock company, audited, and valued, and the SPA solicits other bids. The interested investors have 90 days to respond. If the initiating investor's bid is close to the valuation, that investor has the right of first refusal; otherwise, the investors compete for the firm.

The objective of the SPA privatization program for large enterprises is to bring groups of twenty companies to market about every three or four months. Methods of transferring ownership from the state to private hands include public offerings on stock exchanges, competitive tenders, Employee Stock Option Programs (ESOPs), as well as competitive bidding by investor groups for the right to manage the privatization. This latter method has been termed "privatizing the privatization process," because it relieves the SPA of ownership and of the responsibility of selling or restructuring the enterprise at the very earliest stage.

How much the government should restructure state enterprise prior to sale is an important policy question. Spinning off the auxiliary operations is the least controversial type of restructuring. Breaking down the production facilities is more controversial. On the one hand, more extensive restructuring before privatizing could yield an enterprise that operates more like a private firm. Such a restructured firm also might fetch more when it is privatized. On the other hand, the state has shown no ability in the past to structure firms in an economically rational manner. The Hungarian government appears to be taking an active role in restructuring production units only in the case of large state enterprises that, because of their strategic importance to the economy, are likely to be privatized last.

Foreign direct investment is a third track for developing the private sector in Hungary. A foreign firm picks a market niche, usually investing with majority ownership, and the state facilitates the venture, often through tax holidays. The Hungarian government provides investor services that list domestic companies looking for joint venture partners.

Joint ventures benefit the investor by offering majority control with a smaller investment outlay and by allowing entry into a market niche without the burdens of restructuring associated with the large privatizations. They benefit the country by creating a midsize industry sector that channels Western technology, expertise, contracts, and credit to the most dynamic parts of the economy.

Hungary has had liberal investment laws and attractive tax holidays for foreign investors since 1988, but changes in 1991 were designed to focus government policies more narrowly on higher-valued foreign investment in strategic manufacturing sectors. As of January 1991, government approval is no longer required for majority or 100 percent foreign-owned investment. Full repatriation of profits in the currency of the original investment is allowed. Imports needed for foreign-owned production facilities can enter duty-free. There are no foreign exchange controls, and expropriation requires due legal process and full compensation.

As a further inducement to foreign investment in Hungary, the government set up a 1.5 billion forint ($22 million) investment promotion fund. Awarded quarterly by competitive tender, these funds can be used for infrastructure (roads, pipelines, electricity) development to support joint ventures or in some cases for limited and temporary government investment into the joint venture itself.

Foreign investment funds are another source of private-sector capital. Despite great interest, their impact on the SME sector has been limited, and most have not invested the full amount of capital raised. The First Hungarian Investment Fund was established in 1989 with an authorized capital of $100 million, but its actual capital is estimated at $80 million, and little has actually been invested outside of the London financial centers. The Hungarian Investment Company LTD, founded by British promoters in February 1990, has invested only $20 million of its $100 million. The Hungarian Paribas Corp., Italgenco (part of IRI), and a group of Israeli investors are trying to put together deals, but are apparently finding it difficult to raise interest at the SPA. Cohfin, part of the DiBenedetti Group, has been the most successful, investing about $15 million in the Hungarian markets since May 1990 and acquiring a majority interest in investments totaling about $20 million. What is not clear is why the unsuccessful investors have not participated in the investor-initiated program of privatization.

Creating a Stable and Competitive Environment

A private SME sector only flourishes when the economic environment is stable and competitive. The essential elements of the broad reform programs needed to achieve this goal are fiscal reforms and goods-markets reforms, particularly price liberalization. By reducing pressures for monetary creation, fiscal reforms help establish a stable macroeconomic environment. Price liberalization and trade reforms, including partial external convertibility at a realistic exchange rate, allow relative prices to reflect consumer preferences, production costs, and international comparative advantage, which together encourage competition and efficient resource allocation. Additional reforms necessary for successful SMEs are solid legal and accounting conventions, financial system reforms, and entrepreneurship.

Hungary experimented with partial reforms as long ago as 1968. In 1990, however, the government implemented a far-reaching program that accelerated the pace of price and trade reforms, setting the stage for measures explicitly directed at the SME sector and privatization of state-owned firms. By early 1991, only about 10 percent of prices were regulated—those of certain consumer necessities (such as white bread and milk), household energy, and some rents—compared to 50 percent in 1988. The first two stages of import liberalization in 1989 and 1990 freed 70 percent of imports from trade and exchange restrictions, exposing 32 percent of production to international market competition. Further liberalization in early 1991 raised these percentages to 90 percent of imports and 70 percent of industrial production.

Promoting competition is of particular importance in Hungary for successful growth of SMEs. As prices are liberalized and firms become privately held and managed, oligopoly or monopoly behavior could inhibit entry of new private firms. An appropriate exchange rate and trade liberalization are important checks on monopoly behavior. In addition, a Competition and Cartel Office was established in 1990 to monitor and ensure compliance with the law prohibiting unfair market practices. This new law controls mergers, prohibits unfair competition, and reviews performance of firms with "economic superiority" (defined as 30 percent of more of market share). In particular, the law protects new entrants from differential treatment in the purchase of inputs or sales to distribution outlets by existing firms with economic superiority.

A critical element in the transition to a market-based system is financial system reform. At present, the commercial banks are saddled with nonperforming loans made to state-owned enterprises and have little desire or ability to extend credit to a new SME sector. And there is almost no venture capital or personal wealth to finance small manufacturing operations or to purchase retail outlets or distribution systems as they are spun off from the SOEs. The Hungarian government has responded to these market failures with several preferential credit programs.

This particular problem originated with the "instant" commercialization of the banking system in 1987. Hungary split the state-owned monobank into a central bank with monetary policy responsibilities and three commercial banks that received the outstanding portfolio of enterprise loans and lending responsibilities. These banks were under-capitalized (capital adequacy is around 10 percent) and their portfolios are still concentrated by industry sector. Because of the poor portfolios, the banks cannot lend to new enterprises—available funds are rolled over to existing borrowers to maintain the illusion of solvency. More-over, the situation perpetuates itself, since banks as the main creditors clearly cannot force the bankruptcy of insolvent firms.

A thorough rebuilding of the banking system needs to address both the flow of bad credits and the stock of problem loans. The techniques of credit assessment and prudential regulation are being implemented, but removing the stock of bad loans may be a prerequisite for bankers to act both prudently and entrepreneurially. These reforms will not change the system in the short term, however, so the Hungarian government in the meantime is trying to find the appropriate balance between preferential credit facilities and market-rate facilities to meet the needs of the emerging market economy without a return to centralized pricing, negative real rates, and allocated credit.

Two funds provide preferential credit for the initial purchase of a shop or of capital assets. Loans through the Privatization Credit Facility are somewhat like mortgages. A domestic investor seeking to purchase a state enterprise at auction can leverage his own capital by borrowing against the value of the target state enterprise. Loans through the Exis-tence Fund are more like secured personal loans. Smaller entrepreneurs can use the proceeds to purchase real estate, installations, machines, or inventory at a privatization auction in order to start a new business. The interest rates on both funds are 75 percent of the long-term interest rate, and thus likely to be negative in real terms. Moreover, the National Bank of Hungary absorbs half of the default risk on loans through the Existence Fund. Additional borrowing for working capital needs or ex-pansion is at market interest rates, however. This two-tiered structure attempts to rectify the problem of insufficient wealth in the domestic economy by reducing the entry cost of private investment, but preserves the market test for marginal decisions by both bank and entrepreneur.

Business acumen is understandably a bit rusty, and several groups focusing on the SME sector have sprung up. Within the Ministry of Industry and Trade, the Small Business Administration is working to reduce the impact of government regulations and laws on SMEs and to help them win government procurement contracts. The government is also working to increase information about domestic and foreign market opportunities.

The Hungarian Foundation for Small Enterprise Economic Develop-ment (SEED), which opened its doors in 1990, is one of a number of private nonprofit organizations promoting small business by focusing on technical assistance and education programs. SEED works through the local Chamber of Commerce networks, running seminars on such topics as business plans, marketing, foreign investment, financial management, and consulting. It has also set up five business incubators. These facilities group small businesses together to allow the common use of secretaries, telephones, copying machines, and so forth. As well as reducing costs, however, business incubators bring together entrepreneurs with ideas and promote business networking.

Structural Change in Hungary: The Result So Far

Changes in the legal foundation for private enterprise and the liberalization of the markets have resulted in a boom for private enterprise. More than 16,000 new small firms (fewer than 50 employees) were registered in 1990, more than doubling Hungary's population of small firms and increasing the share of small firms in industrial enterprises from 6 to 9 percent between January and September 1990. These new firms are playing an important role in absorbing labor. Employment by private businesses increased by more than 10,000 last year, out of 90,000 unemployed. A survey conducted by Hungarian statistical authorities estimates that the contribution of small business to industrial output doubled from 6 percent in 1989 to 12 percent in 1990.

Most of the new firms are engaged in trade and construction; since trade did not exist under central planning, there is little competition from the state sector. Private employment in retail and wholesale trade expanded 2-1/2 times from January 1990 to January 1991, while private businesses accounted for some 40 percent of total construction activity in the first half of 1990. With the introduction of the Existence and Privatization Funds, the scale of operations may increase toward the midsize sector.

Hungary faces two external challenges, the collapse of the Communist market trade arrangement and the burden of external debt. Both require increased exports to hard-currency markets, primarily in the industrial countries. And in fact, export performance to non-Communist markets was beyond expectations in 1990 and the first quarter of 1991. Although data are not available indicating whether exports originated from the state or private sector, exports expanded most from industry branches that had not previously been active exporters. This suggests that private entrepreneurs might have entered those sectors and contributed to export performance. Anticipated financial system reforms that provide trade credit enhancements and coverage for foreign exchange risk will help here.

As far as privatization and restructuring of the large SOEs is concerned, there are about 2500 of these with an asset value estimated at $32 billion; about 1000 are manufacturing enterprises. Through March

1991, ten had been sold (seven partially and three fully) for a total value of somewhat less than $100 million. The industries in the two privatization programs so far include several hotel chains, a retail chain, a drug company, a plastics manufacturer, and a scrap recycling firm, as well as several textile and apparel manufacturers, a furniture company, tile works, several different machinery-producing companies, optical works, and a weapons and gas appliances factory.

The SPA has approved between fifty and seventy "spontaneous privatization" joint ventures with total assets of $294 million; foreign participation was 42 percent of share capital. In addition, forty-one outright sales were approved with total asset value of $194 million. The SPA is considering subcontracting the management of its 94 billion forint portfolio of shares in approximately sixty partially privatized companies.

A successful test auction for the so-called Pre-Privatization Program was held in December 1990, but further auctions were put on hold until the legislation governing compensation is passed. Who gets the proceeds and who owns the right to lease land must be clarified.

Hungary estimated total foreign direct investment in place as of late 1990 (as opposed to committed but not yet funded) at $1.2 billion. About $700 million of the total flowed into Hungary in 1990 alone, representing more than one-half of the total foreign direct investment (FDI) flow into East and Central Europe that year. The Hungarian government further estimates that in 1991 FDI will total between $800 million and $1 billion.

The United States is the largest foreign investor in Hungary in value terms (Germany and Austria lead in numbers of deals) and has accounted for about one-half of all foreign investment in Hungary. Major firms involved are GE, Ford, GM, Guardian Industries, Sara Lee, Citibank, Ralston-Purina, and Dow Chemical.

Of the approximately 5000 joint ventures in Hungary, more than half were established in 1990, and most are SMEs. Data for 1989 suggest that the joint ventures were more profitable than the state-owned firms in similar industry branches and accounted for just less than 10 percent of total industry profits earned in the economy. By industry branch, 45 percent were in engineering, and these were the most profitable. Light industry and chemical industry also received foreign capital infusions.

Sectors of emerging interest are tourism, software, and financial consulting and accounting services. About one-third are majority foreign-owned, with somewhat less than one-fourth fully foreign-owned. Early statistics for 1990 are similar, although it appears that the average capitalization dropped between 1989 and 1990 from about $400,000 per firm to about $225,000 per firm, although some of this apparent drop may represent exchange rate changes.

Concluding Observations

Small and midsize enterprises play key roles in production and employment and in the transmission of market signals in market economies. Hence, the economic transformation of ECE would be facilitated by a robust SME sector. The challenge facing the governments of ECE is to create a stable environment in which the small and midsize enterprise sector can thrive. Because central planning was historically biased against the SME sector, government policy explicitly to encourage SMEs is necessary. Policies must be chosen with care to avoid creating a sector of weak enterprises dependent on the government.

Hungary is in a good position to quickly develop a midsize sector. Partial reforms over the last decade or so increased the diversity of firm sizes in the country and created limited market signals. Privatizing the small and midsize industrial cooperatives could create a SME sector instantly. Policies directed specifically at the origination of new private enterprise include the capital funds.

The success of Hungary's (and other countries') efforts depends on broad-based reforms to complete the transition to a market economy and to spread business acumen. Hungary needs to maintain fiscal balance, to keep inflation in check, to complete price and trade liberalization, to move forward on financial sector reforms, and to provide sufficient business advice and education.

Index